What Success Looks Like

What Success Looks Like

Increasing High School Graduation Rates among Males of Color

Marck Abraham

ROWMAN & LITTLEFIELD
Lanham • Boulder • New York • London

Published by Rowman & Littlefield
An imprint of The Rowman & Littlefield Publishing Group, Inc.
4501 Forbes Boulevard, Suite 200, Lanham, Maryland 20706
www.rowman.com

6 Tinworth Street, London SE11 5AL, United Kingdom

British Library Cataloguing in Publication Information Available

Library of Congress Cataloging-in-Publication Data

Names: Abraham, Marck, 1984- author.
Title: What success looks like : increasing high school graduation rates among males of
    color / Marck Abraham.
Description: Lanham, Maryland : Rowman & Littlefield, [2021] | Includes
    bibliographical references and index. | Summary: "Black males have the lowest
    graduation rates of any population in the country, graduating from high school at
    the rate of just 59%. They are suspended and referred to special education classes
    at rates three times higher than any other population. They make up just 6% of the
    US population yet account for nearly a third of the American prison population.
    The graduation gap between White and Black males is currently 21% and growing.
    Research has shown that costly federal, state, and local programs have failed to
    solve this crisis. This book details the 10-step method I developed and deployed
    in the Buffalo (New York) high school of which I was principal, which has raised
    the four-year graduation rate for Black males to 93% and the five-year rate to 90%.
    My program has been deployed throughout New York State and I am now advising
    schools nationally, helping them to deploy proven strategies that will guarantee
    the academic success of Black males. This is a one-of-a-kind book with powerful
    strategies secondary and middle school principals can use to transform their entire
    school. The strategies in this book are what every successful principal needs to run
    a high performing school. This book answers the age-old question: "Can principals
    truly make a difference and turn their school around?" The answer is yes, they can!
    This book will show them how"— Provided by publisher.
Identifiers: LCCN 2021014214 (print) | LCCN 2021014215 (ebook) |
    ISBN 9781475861075 (cloth) | ISBN 9781475861099 (ebook)
    ISBN 9781475861082 (paper)
Subjects: LCSH: African American boys—Education (Secondary) | High school
    graduates—United States—Statistics. | High schools—United States—Graduation
    requirements. | Academic achievement—United States. | School principals—United
    States. | Educational change—United States.
Classification: LCC LC2779 .A37 2021 (print) | LCC LC2779 (ebook) |
    DDC 371.829/96073—dc23
LC record available at https://lccn.loc.gov/2021014214
LC ebook record available at https://lccn.loc.gov/2021014215

♾™ The paper used in this publication meets the minimum requirements of American
National Standard for Information Sciences—Permanence of Paper for Printed Library
Materials, ANSI/NISO Z39.48-1992.

Contents

Preface

This is a professional book by a professional educator. It identifies a crisis in American education, namely, the yawning gap that separates high school graduation rates for Black males from the rates for every other student group in our nation. Historically, this gap has resisted all efforts to bridge or close it. This book offers a pragmatic solution validated by results.

But to understand the solution presented here, you need to know the context in which it is approached. That means you need to know something about the origin of this book, which is personal. So, please, indulge me for a few pages so that I can tell you who I am and how I came to write this book.

My name is Marck Abraham. I was born in Carol City, a neighborhood in Miami Gardens, Florida, a place of notable crime and poverty. My family is from Haiti, so I'm a first-generation American, one of four children, the son of Lilly and (I believed, growing up) Frank Abraham. Mom brought us up to the best of her ability. Frank Abraham was a very strict father and an abusive man, who beat my mom routinely, and he called me stupid so often that I thought it was part of my name. Ours was a house smoldering with anxiety. You never knew when a fight would break out. You just knew it *would*.

School was in some ways an escape from home, but I always carried with me to class a lot of what I got at home. If you're called stupid, you come to believe you are stupid, and in school you spend more time second-guessing yourself than you do learning. I was in second or third grade when my mother acted on what was for her the last straw. Frank Abraham called my sister a bitch. Well, it seems mom had been secretly putting money away and had enough to put down on a house in Hollywood, Florida. She loaded up a rented van and took us all with her. To this day, it remains the most daring and courageous thing I ever personally witnessed.

Hollywood in Broward County was a step up from Carol City in Dade, even though it was a major challenge for mom to be a single working mother with four small children. As for us kids, you could take the child out of Carol City, but it's not so easy to take Carol City out of the child. We were like these hood kids, and we started stealing everything that wasn't nailed down—bikes, toys, you name it, shoplifting included.

Hollywood did bring change to me, though. My mom introduced me to a Haitian guy named Michelle. A smooth brother with a rich Haitian accent, he could light up a room with his amazing smile and laughter. Months after I met him, mom revealed that he, not Frank Abraham, was my birth father. Now, Frank Abraham had hit me, whipped me, and called me stupid. But he was—or had been—my dad, and I couldn't stop crying. By way of consolation, all my mother offered was a command: "Stop crying."

Michelle came around to the house a few times after my mother's revelation but then disappeared, and I distracted myself with my new school in Broward County. It was way better than what I had experienced in Dade County, and I was even recommended for honors classes. Having grown up with a man who called me stupid, the recommendation excited me. But when they sat me down for an interview, the teachers asked me questions I just couldn't answer. For example, they showed me a picture of an escalator in a shopping mall.

"What is this called?"

"Oh, those are the stairs," I answered. Easy one! And then, for good measure, I added, "That move."

I didn't make it into the honors classes. Why? Because at that time, I had never visited a shopping mall. I knew that there were moving stairs out in the world, but I had never actually used them, and the word *escalator* had simply never come up in the life I led.

Not getting into those honor classes was disappointing, but it was a lesson I never forgot: the failure that excluded me out was not mine. It was the school's, whose teachers lacked cultural proficiency, the ability to recognize how culture shapes experience and how experience shapes understanding, knowledge, and vocabulary. We are a diverse nation. One size does not fit all.

I learned that lesson that very day, and, as a school principal, I made it my business to exercise that awareness every day.

In Hollywood, I made friends. There was Ty, who lived across the street, and there was Steve, down the street from me. We became best friends, the three of us. And then I made a lot more friends, playing basketball and football. I was not as close to them as I was to Ty and Steve, but I really admired some of them, especially those who played sports hard and well. And that was good, because, after I was passed over for honors classes, most of the teachers were none too encouraging. I didn't fail any grades, but I had this teacher—let's call her Miss Smith—who took me back to the reign of Frank Abraham, when she would say the most ridiculously insulting things to me: "Hey, you're so dumb your brain must be smaller than a retarded gnat."

Looking back at that as an adult and an educator, it is clear to me that the woman had no business being a teacher—though her choice of vocation may have been the least of her problems. What does it say about a grown woman who punches down at children like that? But, at the time she said it, being called dumb and stupid, well, I was pretty numb to it. That was about the time my buddy Steve and I went into the school library to look up the word *Black*. Nobody told us to do it, and it seems to me kind of a weird thing to do in fourth grade, but we wanted to see what the word, which was applied to us all the time, really meant—officially.

What we found was bad. Everything negative was associated with *Black*. Right? We read the definitions in a dictionary so big and thick it had its own lectern to hold it. The words were horrible. *Darkest color, absence of light, reflecting or transmitting little or no light, opposite of white, deeply stained with dirt, characterized by tragic or disastrous events, causing despair or pessimism, full of gloom or misery, depressed, full of anger or hatred, indicative of condemnation or discredit, very evil or wicked*, and, for good measure, *connected with the devil.*

Well, at least I knew why I was the way I was. It was all right there in the dictionary. So, for one thing, I kept right on stealing. My first pair of Reeboks? I stole them. Walked into a store, left them my old beat-up shoes, and walked out with new Reeboks. Then the management got smart and started putting out on display just one shoe at a time. I don't think it was all because of me. I doubt I was the only one lifting shoes. And while that one-shoe tactic was a highly effective deterrent in a shoe store, there were plenty of other shops to hit.

I was a thief for longer than I like to admit, but what began to change my criminal trajectory and even put me on the path to college was not antitheft measures in a shoe store. It was football.

I got into it when I was eleven, early in middle school. I was a big kid, and so I was playing with high school-age kids, an eleven-year-old playing tackle with sixteen-year-olds. It was tough, and it was punishing, but there were rules, discipline, and *coaches*. Most of all, there were teams. Now, I'm not saying I had a magical transformation. Far from it. In my seventh- and eighth-grade years, I feel like I probably skipped school every other day. I was a straight-up truant. I didn't go to class. I mean, I might go Monday and Tuesday, skip Wednesday, show up for part of Thursday, and blow off Friday altogether. To this day, I don't even know how I passed.

I wasn't alone. There was a truant officer we used to call Robocop, and if he caught you, he'd haul you off to juvenile. But we didn't get caught. Evasion required no criminal genius. We'd just say we had missed the bus. And that seemed to be answer enough. The teachers? I don't think they even bothered with taking attendance. As for mom, she never knew I wasn't in school. There was no meaningful communication between school and home.

And the other thing was that, delinquent though I might be, I was never disrespectful. Because school wasn't hard for me, I managed to crank out the B's and the C's. As I figured it, the *game* of school was that if you're the kid who's charming and don't really cause anybody trouble, you're not cursing anybody out, nobody's really very concerned about you. So, much of the time, I hung out with my guys, smoked our Black & Milds, which were big in Black communities, cigars machine-rolled with pipe tobacco, went to girls' houses, and it was basically rock and roll.

Football was another thing altogether. I *always* showed up to practice. It was an after-school thing, and it was not a school program but a community-based program, a community-sponsored team, the Hollywood Hills Little League Football team. I think it maybe saved my life.

Not that I had any special talent at football. I was clumsy, and while I was bigger than other kids my age, I was playing against sixteen-year-olds, most of them bigger than I was. But I had this coach. Coach Choppy was the kind of man a lot of boys, especially Black boys, need in their lives. He was demanding, but he always encouraged me and took me under his wing and told me I was special and, most of all, told me that I had a bright future.

Then came one day in practice—I think I was twelve by this time, my second year playing Little League—when we were visited by a young man, a white guy, who was playing for a Division Two or Three college team. He told us—and I remember it word for word—"You guys can get a scholarship and go to college *for free* if you play football. *Like me.*"

Now, here I was a kid who was skipping school more than half the time, and all I could think was *What? I can go to college for free!* Football gets you free college. It was a revelation, a lightning bolt, and a Burning Bush rolled into one. So, I told Ty and Steve that I was going to *play* and go to college for free.

Bam! That was it. I kept playing. I made it out of middle school and into high school and was about to learn that the difference between the two was that in high school, they seriously kept score. Performance counted, and performance was cumulative. The days of skating by were over.

Just before I moved on to high school, my mother was getting with a new guy named Reggie. He was cool. As a strong male figure in my life, Reggie was the closest thing I had to Coach Choppy. He made a commitment, became my stepdad, and nobody had to tell me to call him dad. He was a man with self-respect and respect for others and with a genuine entrepreneurial vision. Another Haitian immigrant, he was a go-getter, into real estate and miscellaneous other stuff, all focused on making money. He started flipping houses, beginning with ours. He moved us, sold the house, and made a pretty penny on it.

But this meant that we moved about forty-five minutes away, and I ended up going to a different high school from my friends and teammates, including Ty and Steve, though we kept in touch by cellphone. About midway through my sophomore year in high school, Steve, with whom I used to skip school, was arrested, accused of involvement with somebody who shot somebody else. They charged and tried Steve as an adult—presumably as an accessory to murder—and he went to prison for six or eight years. Just like that, he disappeared from my life, and I wouldn't hear from him again for years.

That was my introduction to the school-to-prison pipeline. For too many Black males, if you couldn't graduate, if you dropped out, or drifted out, you ended up in a world of criminal activity that led to incarceration—or even worse.

As for me, I wanted to stay in high school as long as I could keep playing football, especially after the coach told me, "A guy your size, big as you are, you're going to play Division 1 college football. Period." I didn't know what that meant, exactly, except that it sounded like it meant I was going to college for free. But the coach told me that I had to maintain my grades at a certain level to stay on the team. So, I was motivated.

In fact, I promised myself that I would give it 100 percent. But I have to admit that my 100 percent only got me out of high school with something like 800 on my SATs. Honestly, I was practically illiterate. And I wasn't the best football player, either. By senior year, I wasn't number one or anything close to it, but I was very big, and I did play football. So, senior year, I found myself with fifteen, sixteen, or seventeen scholarship offers on the table. I chose SUNY Buffalo.

I graduated and left semi-tropical southern Florida for semi-Arctic western New York. I'm nineteen, alone in Buffalo, when the phone rings at three in the morning. On the other end of the line was the Miami PD.

"Is this Marck Abraham?"

"Yes."

"Uh, well, I'm sorry to inform you, but somebody just killed your dad."

It was not Frank Abraham they were talking about and not Reggie. It was Michelle, my biological father. His end came just as he had drifted back into my orbit and we were getting into some kind of a groove that at least resembled a relationship. That was important. That was hopeful. Because I was grappling with the question of what was wrong with me that caused this man not to love me. What was wrong with me, that this person didn't think I was special enough to have any part in my life?

They were questions that would eventually guide my approach, as an educator, to working with young Black male students. I understood that they needed a strong male presence in their lives, and, often, it was not something they were getting from within their own family. But, for now, all I could think of was how my best friend Steve was in prison and Michelle was dead.

So, who was *I*? And where was *I* going?

My freshman year at Buffalo was rough, ending with a 1.6 GPA. When I had moved from Carol City to Hollywood, from Dade County to Broward, kids told me I talked like a white guy. So, I worked hard to assimilate to their standard of Black culture. Now, years later, at age nineteen, I was in an essentially all-white university, a "research 1" institution, meaning that its professors did research at the highest levels. I tried to fall back on what had worked for me in elementary school, middle school, and, to some extent, even high school, turning on the charm, smiling, being a nice guy, respectful, and never rocking the boat. At SUNY Buffalo, that wasn't cutting it. Everybody expected you to do the work.

I remember the first paper I turned in for a class. I stumbled from the get-go. I stumbled on the word *the*, which I spelled "da." I couldn't spell. Worse, I couldn't really write. The paper came back from the professor with so much red ink on it that I was too embarrassed to return to his class. I dropped it. Of course, the problem applied to more than one class. I had wasted much of my schooling, and although football was paying my way, I had a much bigger deficit to make up. I didn't read, so I could hardly read. I didn't write, so I could hardly write. I soon found myself on academic probation.

Now, when I started at Buffalo, I was the only true freshman playing as a freshman. As in Little League, an eleven-year-old playing among sixteen-year-olds, I was getting banged up. Except now the guys were *much* bigger and *much* better. I was nineteen pitted against twenty-four and twenty-five-year-olds. Injury became a way of life, and I started taking painkillers before the game, in the game, and after the game just so I could function.

So, I was in a game when I ran and jumped over one person, not even six inches off the ground. I jumped, came down hard on the ground and twisted my ankle, which blew up to about the size of my head. The next week, I had to have surgery on my shoulder. After these things, my passion for football, which *had* saved my life, drained out and oozed away. I had the skills, but I just couldn't play. I no longer had the passion for it.

It was at this point, my lowest point, a point where I was drifting into failure at school and now had lost my passion for football and was questioning my very identity, that I found fellowship in the church.

Now, I had gone to church as a kid, and I had learned to pray. I would pray to God before every game to help me win. And when, instead, I just got hurt,

I stopped praying. Now, in a new church with a new pastor, I started again. This time, my prayer was, *God, show me how to write.*

At this time, I also discovered the charismatic Pastor Creflo Dollar, whose CDs I bought and listened to over and over again. It suddenly occurred to me to start writing down the Creflo Dollar sermons I listened to. I took down every word. I did it over and over again. I would listen to the audio, pause it, write it, and move ahead to the next bit.

One thing about an effective sermon—it's good writing. It's a persuasive argument. It makes sense and it moves people. So, waxing on and waxing off hour after hour and day by day, I learned how to spell, how to write, but most of all, I learned how to create a persuasive argument, from thesis statement to conclusion. My grades began to climb, slowly, and my health improved.

I graduated from Buffalo with a 2.0 GPA and set about making a living. I married and, barely two years later, divorced. Not long after this event, I got a call from Florida.

"Somebody killed Steve."

Steve!

I had lost touch with him after he went off to prison until he called me when I was a sophomore at Buffalo, about two years before this phone call. I had been stunned to hear from him because, in a way, he was already dead to me. Gone. So, it was something like a call from the Other Side.

"Oh, what's good?" I managed to say. "What're you doin'?"

"Man, I'm just sittin' in the trap."

At the time, I didn't even know what "the trap" meant.

"You don't know what the trap is, man? Drug dealing."

"Oh . . . cool," I said. But I was thinking, your world is not *my* world. I'm playing football, and I'm on national TV. I knew we had parted ways. Not intentionally. It's just how it happened. He went off to prison. I stayed in high school, played football, and football got me into college. No sooner did he get out of jail than he started dealing drugs. His life, which used to be just like my life back when we were skipping school together to smoke Black & Milds, was now so far from my life that we didn't even speak the same language anymore. I was struggling through college, getting serious about the church, and just trying to do the best I could. Steve was "in the trap."

About two years after I learned that Steve had been murdered, I got another call. This time it was about Ty, my other best friend from Florida days.

Ty had gotten into big trouble in our junior year in high school, when he was charged with rape. The charge stuck, he was tried, convicted, and sent off to "big people" jail. He didn't get out until *my* senior year in college, when I actually met up with him. He started talking about some religious stuff, but it didn't seem real to me.

The next thing I heard after that meeting came by phone. A mutual friend called to tell me that, as a registered sex offender, Ty had been required to report to his parole officer regularly. When he didn't show up one day, the PO violated him, and he fled to Georgia. Florida never found out where he went. Didn't much care that a Florida sex offender was now Georgia's problem. In Georgia, he just tried to get by. He went to a house to buy some weed, and the guy at the door tried to rob him. Ty turned around to leave and got shot point-blank in the back.

When I started at SUNY Buffalo, I was a business major. I began to realize more and more that I just hated it. For one thing, I was failing economics. You even say the word "macroeconomics" to me today, and I just start falling asleep. It was after Ty was killed, the second of my two best friends from childhood to die violently, that I switched my major to sociology and African American history. I was looking to prepare for a teaching career.

I didn't make that decision just because I couldn't stand my business major. I saw my two best friends go to jail and then get killed. These guys were brilliant. I mean it. These guys were also great athletes—much better than I was. *They* could have been on football scholarships. *They* could have excelled in college and in life. But they never finished high school.

I know this is "anecdotal evidence"—two young Black men close to me who committed crimes and who died young, both of them murdered. But they were my best friends, and, like them, I was a young Black male. Still, I lived, and they didn't. I graduated from high school. They didn't.

Anecdotal evidence or not, I did the math. Later, I would discover the statistics: males of all races and ethnicities who leave high school without a diploma had a mortality rate between ages thirty-nine and forty-six, over twice that of high school graduates. Male Black high school dropouts in this same age group had the highest death rate of all: 11.6 percent compared to 7.8 percent for Black males with a diploma.[1]

But I didn't need statistics to do my own back-of-the-envelope calculation. If you are Black and male, there's a good chance you won't finish high school. And if you are Black and male and don't finish high school, there's a good chance you'll die young. Finishing high school doesn't guarantee an easy life, of course. After high school, I continued to struggle in learning to read and write and speak so that people would listen to me. I played football through injury after injury to pay for my education. But I took that education very far beyond where I ever dreamed I could go: a bachelor's, two masters, a doctorate. All were costly, one way or another, but I never had a moment's doubt that it was all worth it.

I had a mission. It was far more specific than educating young people. It was specifically to lift high school graduation rates. More specifically, the mission in my head and my heart was to get more Black young men to cross the stage at commencement time. That, I understood, was a matter of life or death.

After clawing my way from near-illiteracy to a high school diploma and a body-punishing football scholarship to SUNY Buffalo, I started studying to become a teacher but soon discovered that my sense of mission was better served by preparation in counseling. Through that training, I moved into administration, which is where I focused my doctoral studies. After getting my BA at SUNY Buffalo in Sociology and African American History in 2008, I earned an MS in Counseling and Human Services from Canisius College in Buffalo in 2010, and another MS in Educational Administration and Supervision from the same place in 2013. My doctorate, an EdD in Executive Leadership, was awarded in 2019 by Saint John Fisher College, in Rochester.

In the meantime, in 2014 I joined the staff of Buffalo's McKinley Vocational High School as dean of students and, later that year, was appointed as an assistant principal. In May 2017, a McKinley senior filed a federal lawsuit against the Buffalo school district, alleging that the principal at the time and other school officials barred him from forming an after-school club for gay and lesbian students. In addition, LGBTQ students were also warned against bringing same-sex dates to the prom. The principal was identified as the moving force behind what the suit called a pattern of discriminatory actions against LGBTQ students.

With school suddenly embroiled in a contentious suit and a public controversy, the principal was put on leave, and I was appointed acting principal with barely a week's lead time and in the middle of what had become a national scandal.

McKinley High School was in turbulence, with the media flying around us in a whirlwind. I was just trying to hold us together. It was already May, and, as I saw it, my first job was to keep my head down and just get us to and through graduation in June. We got there, and then the summer of 2017 came and went, and I was still acting principal when the new school year started in the fall.

By that time, I was in the middle of heavy doctoral research on the issue of Black male academic underperformance and dismal graduation rates. As McKinley dean of students and assistant principal, I had already begun introducing initiatives aimed at increasing our graduation rates, and the June 2017 graduating class did show a very significant spike in numbers, especially among Black male students. I led summer school, and now, with the new school year, I would no longer lie low but intended to take full advantage of my accountability as acting principal by building on our emerging success to take my initiatives to scale.

Back in June, I had talked with the whole McKinley staff about the importance of telling our story *ourselves*, of controlling the message *we* wanted to send. In June, the media narrative had been about two things: that we had a principal who hates gay people and that we were a subpar, underperforming failure of a school. So, as acting principal, the accountable leader of the school, I put on a full-court press through social media. I got everybody on the same page to broadcast *our* story. We started a Facebook page, a Twitter account, and an Instagram account, and I got a dedicated staff member at the district to take charge of the social media. My mission was to relentlessly post positive material.

It started to work. We built a wave which grew steadily, a couple of thousand people at first, and then our videos began drawing up to 35,000 views. I continued to build on what I had started as assistant principal. As dean of students my immediate administrative focus had been the seniors. Confronting their dismal graduation rate, I did what needed to be done to help them get over the line. I was going to their houses to talk with them and their families. During the school day, I'd go through the neighborhood and pull truants out of stores and off the corners. I counseled. And when the district made me acting principal, I started bringing the whole thing up to scale.

Still, the local press focused on the scandal that just would not go away. For ten months, most of the news that reached the community was negative. Ten months of bad news is practically an eternity, but it was also a span in which the graduation-rate program I was scaling up began showing results. In the teeth of the storm, an official report was issued on graduation rates in New York State. It revealed that, under my leadership, McKinley was producing an exceptional rate of Black male graduation, which was not only higher than every other school in the state but significantly higher than most schools in the nation.

Those results pulled both me and McKinley High School back from the brink. I had shown both McKinley and the state of New York what success looked like. I intended to go on to show the nation. I was ready to spread the word: school principals matter.

Part I

LIFE, DEATH, AND DIPLOMAS

Chapter 1

School Principals Matter

Share the Love but Own the Data

Common sense, which often amounts to popular opinion uncritically accepted, makes teachers accountable for the quality of education, including as that quality is measured by high school graduation rates. Of course, teachers play an important role, but the role of school principals is typically minimized and often overlooked entirely.

The fact is that school principals matter. Research shows that a principal's vision and strong leadership are key to creating a school environment that fosters high academic success.[1] By the numbers, principals emerge as a vital factor in increasing student achievement, second only to teachers.[2]

As far back as the 1980s, studies have been conducted at the elementary level to examine the importance of principals in influencing student achievement, teacher development, and school culture.[3] We have ample evidence that successful schools have a principal who is involved with instruction, has a purpose and a clear vision for where the school is going, and shares a belief that all students can learn. As the school leader, principals are key to creating a culture of success.[4]

Formal studies of the impact of principals in high schools, as opposed to elementary schools, are almost nonexistent. I believe, however, that we can extrapolate from the elementary school experience, and we can also look at high schools that have been, in recent years, creating high achievement among Black males. High school principals are at the helm of the culture in their schools. It is possible for school principals to transform negative stereotypes about Black males into positive outcomes. One example is the Eagle

Academy, a New York City charter school, where the principal led Black males to a graduation rate of 84 percent.[5]

Likewise, at Urban Prep Academy in Chicago, the school principal led Black male students to a 100 percent graduation rate, with 100 percent of those graduates achieving acceptance to college. As of 2016, Urban Prep Academy had been producing these results for seven years.[6]

The research reveals that it is the principals who must lead reform within their schools and that the sense of urgency in this must come from them.[7] It is within the principal's power to create a safe and accepting culture, which makes all students feel welcome. Schools that are closing the achievement gap among minority students are led by strong and courageous principals, who have a sense of urgency to do something different within the culture of their buildings. Successful schools look inward for ways to increase student achievement among their minority populations. In contrast, unsuccessful schools typically have a culture that blames students and parents for student failure.[8]

With opportunity for influence comes accountability for performance. Government initiatives such as Race to the Top, No Child Left Behind, and the Every Student Succeeds Act hold principals accountable to ensure all students achieve academically, yet the guidance in cultural proficiency, the skillset principals must acquire to ensure that they understand the diversity of cultures within their own schools, is often lacking. It is important to study all student achievement, but it is imperative that data for minority subgroups, especially Black males, are analyzed and understood.

A 2012 study indicated a need for reform in urban schools, especially for improving performance among Black males, who, as a group, are failing at a high rate.[9] Already, principals in some states have been finding success with this subgroup. In New Jersey and Tennessee, some secondary school principals are doing a phenomenal job and are finding ways to graduate Black males at a rate above the dismal national average of 59 percent.[10] Their success gives the lie to uncritical assumptions that principals don't much matter and that Black males cannot be successful.

My mission came into being when I saw my friends drop out, go to prison, and die. So, how could high school principals—like me—achieve success with increasing the graduation rate among male students of color? Solid and encouraging performance data from elementary schools exists, but, in many ways elementary and secondary education are different worlds. Much more self-motivation and self-reliance are required of high school students. Moreover, despite many efforts and billions of dollars in resources devoted to closing the high school performance and graduation gap between White and Black students—especially Black male students—that gap has actually been increasing since the 1980s.[11]

To understand how principals can work to close the *performance and graduation gap* in high schools, the *research gap* between the elementary and secondary levels in assessing the role of principals must first be closed.

We need to answer three key questions:

1. What, if any, leadership strategies are secondary school principals using in successful schools to increase student achievement among Black males?
2. For those strategies identified, how are they being implemented, and how might they be replicated in other schools?
3. What, if any, aspects of culturally proficient leadership are being employed by successful principals?

From the answers to these very questions have emerged ten steps all dedicated principals can use to lead their schools to higher Black male graduation rates. Does the program work? The response a modest academic would make is *Results are encouraging, but we need more research.* Well, we do need more data. We can never have enough data. But at McKinley High School and other schools that have adopted it, the ten-step program outlined in this book has worked. That is, implementing the program demonstrates that a dedicated principal can create the conditions that increase Black male graduation rates—dramatically. Time will tell how many lives this not only enriches but saves.

LOVE AND DATA

Love and data. Principals need both to lift graduation rates, especially among the group most at risk, Black males.

Sound simple? It is—conceptually. But, like a lot of simple concepts—planting a garden, say—it requires hard work, dedication, and not a little faith. Based on interviews with principals in urban high schools, we find that the high-performing principals are unstintingly generous in the love they gave their students, and they are also zealous about gathering, studying, and generally owning their data.

What We Mean by "Love"

In schools most at risk, when it comes to graduation rates, love calls for understanding and that, in turn, requires adapting to diversity.[12] Mrs. Michelle, principal of Dennis Vocational High School, used a professional development (PD) program to transform the staff's mindset. Students from the school's diversity club led a half-dozen different workshops on such cultural issues as "what it means to be an exchange student, what it means to be an African American student, how . . . it feels to be a woman of Islam." Two other principals, Mr. Wade of Mariah Technical High School and Mr. Jordan of Mia Central High School, partnered with New York University to assist in helping to celebrate diversity. "We had a lot of services come in to help us," Mr. Wade explained. "And we got to this harmony where we are now in a place where everyone gets along . . . now we are this huge community that celebrates diversity."

For schools like those of Mrs. Michelle and Mr. Wade, appreciation of diversity led to culturally responsive teaching, which acknowledges, responds to, and celebrates cultural diversity and sets out to include all students' cultural references in all aspects of learning.

In addition to cultural responsiveness, loving your students calls for rethinking traditional punitive approaches to discipline. Restorative disciplinary practices emphasize the resolution of conflict rather than simply punishing the results. "Victims" and "offenders," together with other concerned parties, are brought together to address an offense of wrongdoing. The objective is to enable all sides to understand the others.

Traditionally, for instance, a student who acted out might be reprimanded with detention or ISS. These are acts of rejection, which do nothing to address the issues and feelings involved in the behavior. A better approach is to ask the student "What happened?" and "How do you feel about what happened?" After this, questions might focus on prompting the student to see his or her action from the point of view of others: "How do you think that outburst made others feel?"

Restorative practices are not about giving a pass to disruptive, objectionable, or inappropriate behavior. Quite the contrary, they are about restoring the social compact between the student who misbehaved and those affected by the misbehavior. It is about understanding, reparation, and forgiveness on all sides. The caring involved, the refusal simply to reject the student, is a demonstration of love.

It takes time and effort. Both Mrs. Michelle and Mr. Jordan (Mia Central High School) instituted special professional training in restorative practices for their staff.

Love is simple, but it requires work.

To take responsibility for every student in a school is to show them love. High school principals who achieve significant improvement in graduation rates all embrace the paradigm that every student in their schools belongs to them. As Mr. Wade put it, "They're all our kids. I don't care what color, what religion, what they wear here, I do not care. They're our kids." Mrs. Etchika, principal of Duplessy-Johnson High School, remarked: "Whether they be male, female, Black, White, Chinese, whatever, it's just the same. Attention is given, in terms of making them feel comfortable, making them feel loved, and cared about, and letting them know that they can achieve, and do whatever it is they want to do with their life and that we're here to support them."

Mrs. Etchika also singled out Black males for mentoring, for a level of attention that makes them "feel comfortable . . . loved and cared about, and [that lets] them know that they can achieve, and do whatever it is they want to do with their life." She said she wanted these students especially to know "that we're here to support them. I think most of all, they really want to feel that they matter."

Showing love is also as simple as doing what Mrs. Michelle does with her students, saying "hello to every kid, doesn't matter who they are. Every kid you pass in the hallway, you talk to, and you say hello to. You go into classrooms to interact with kids."

Simple, yes, but it requires thought, thoughtfulness, and effort, especially to do it consistently. And that's important. Get your students accustomed to being greeted and spoken to, and they will be grateful—unless you slack off or forget!

In fact, take even more time, more effort. Talk to the *families* of your students. As Mrs. Etchika advised: "talk to [the families of your foreign-born students] and ask them questions about what their life was like?" Make time to allow students themselves to tell their stories.

The rewards of the work principals and staff devote to achieving cultural proficiency are evident not only in better graduation numbers but also in enriched experience for educators and students alike. As Mrs. Johnson, principal of Emanuel Honors High School, reported, valuing cultural diversity is "a great advantage. I think it's a phenomenal thing. I think that because when we are talking about students, our kids, and we're preparing for them to go out into the world. What better way to prepare them than for them to be next to a huge diverse [population]?"

"I think our kids are a little more prepared because they've been dealing with diversity since kindergarten—and culture and different cultures," Mr. Wade remarked. "And our school does do a good job at doing different things to keep people together. And I say that at every graduation, our kids are at an advantage because of where they go. We're very eclectic, we're very diverse, and this is what the real world is like."

High-performing principals love their students. Let's put this more precisely. Principals who significantly improve graduation rates in their schools decide that every student in the building belongs to them. This degree of love calls for understanding, which, in turn—and especially in an urban school—demands that principals, teachers, and students adapt to diversity by appreciating and celebrating diversity. In teachers, this mindset leads to culturally responsive teaching, which endeavors to embrace all students' cultural references in all aspects of learning. Discipline remains important, but loving your students requires reforming outmoded punitive approaches and emphasizes resolution of conflict over punishment. With these principles of love uppermost in mind, we turn to the subject of data.

The Data

People talk a lot about left brain versus right brain. They will tell you that "left brain" folks think in words, favor sequencing and linear thinking, are good at math, prize facts, and are rigorously logical. In contrast, those who lean on their "right brain" rely on feelings and visualization more than words, prefer imagination to rigid sequence, and follow intuition more than linear thought. Instead of mathematics, they're into rhythm. Facts are too cut and dry for them. They like to think holistically, and instead of logic, they're into arts.

There is some truth to this. Without question, people have different cognitive styles. But a lot of people take left brain/right brain differences to extremes. True, the human brain does have two hemispheres, but it's still *one* brain in *one* person. Using left-brain skills doesn't mean you have to abandon those in the right brain and vice versa.

Most people are either right-handed or left-handed, but right-handers also use their left hand—a lot. And no southpaw would *literally* give his right arm for anything. So, even if *your* right brain is dominant, you likely still admit the value of tracking your expenses versus your income or being aware of the time of day or day of the month. And you, left-brainer, still love your mother and your kids and even enjoy music with a good beat.

So, let's say *love* is mostly a right-brain thing. But how can we know it works wonders in creating success among culturally diverse high school students? Because we can use our left brain to crunch the *numbers*.

It is all about love *and* data. Educators better saddle up both sides of their brains.

The research in this book was conducted during the author's doctoral work at St. John Fisher College, using a purposeful sampling model to select school principals for what is known as a qualitative phenomenological study—a method of precise description and analysis.

Six principals were chosen for the interviews. They were principals of urban schools or schools close to urban centers that awarded Local, Regents, and Advanced Regents diplomas and whose Black male students were graduating at rates exceeding the New York State average of 63 percent. Data obtained from the New York State Education Department website (New York State Education at a Glance) was used to find the graduation rates and select principals from successful schools—defining "success" not based on such factors as school spirit, student's math scores, English scores, and parental involvement, but on higher-than-average graduation rates for Black males.

The instrument used in working with the six principals was a semistructured interview approach, judged most effective for understanding the issues from the perspective of the principals themselves, from *their* lived experiences. The objective was to understand and evaluate the strategies the principals were using to increase the graduation rates of Black males. I wanted to identify the factors, or themes, common to them all that were proving so successful.

Interview questions deliberately included elements of a culturally proficient leadership perspective. This leadership approach seeks to understand the culture of the students and also to understand them as individuals. Culturally proficient leadership consists of five essential elements: assessing culture, valuing diversity, managing the dynamics of difference, adapting to diversity, and institutionalizing cultural knowledge. The controlling theoretical assumption was that these elements would prove to be key to each principal's success. The presence or absence of the elements guided me in creating a priori codes, which assisted in data analysis. It enabled me to translate inherently subjective qualitative data into more objectively meaningful numbers.

To minimize researcher bias, no data was used from the author's school, and the questions asked were developed collaboratively with an administrative colleague. The confidentiality of the participants was protected by the use of pseudonyms for both them and their schools, and other security measures were taken in gathering, analyzing, and storing the data I collected.

Interviews were recorded and professionally transcribed. To better interpret the data, two standard coding methods were used, emotion coding and in vivo coding.[13] A priori codes—including "school culture"—were created to harmonize the study and to directly answer my research questions.[14]

The emotion coding was used to evaluate the intrapersonal and interpersonal experiences and actions relating to the principals' reasoning, decision-making, and judgments toward Black males. Once the emotion in play was defined, so-called analytic memoing—concise ongoing note-taking of my interpretations—was employed to determine what stories the emotion codes were telling.

In parallel with the emotion coding, vivo coding was used to capture the literal meaning of the principals' experiences in working with the Black males in their schools. Using both the impressionistic emotion coding and the literal in vivo coding enabled analysis of the words each participant used as well as the emotions behind them. After completing two cycles of coding, pattern coding was applied to group interviewer summaries and observations into themes expressed through categorical thematic codes.

FINDINGS

Answers were sought to three research questions:

1. What, if any, leadership strategies are secondary school principals using in successful schools to increase student achievement among Black males?

2. For those strategies identified, how are they being implemented, and how might they be replicated in other schools?
3. What, if any, aspects of culturally proficient leadership are being employed by successful principals?

Each principal was asked these questions, together with a set of follow-up questions to each of the main research questions. The answers were transcribed and then individually coded with eighty-seven codes assigned across the six transcripts. By analyzing the codes, I derived the themes and subthemes that emerged across all the interviews. The six schools varied significantly in size, and the extent of experience of the six principals also varied widely, from sixteen years to 1.5. Nevertheless, there were many striking similarities in the shared experiences of the principals related to increasing graduation rates for Black males.

Research Question 1

What, if any, leadership strategies are secondary school principals using in successful schools to increase student achievement among Black males?

All principals responded with strategies that increased graduation rates for all students, including Black males. Three overarching themes emerged from their responses.

First, *keep everybody on track*, which included a subtheme, *you've got to own it.*

Second, *we care*. These principals created a caring culture for their students. This theme encompassed four subthemes:

1. *make school fun again*
2. *diversity is celebrated, not tolerated*
3. *student voice*
4. *staff are valued*

Third, *clear discipline*. This theme revealed that successful secondary school principals valued discipline within their school. The subtheme associated with clear discipline was *hug it out.*

Keep everybody on track. The principals independently agreed that graduation was the most important task at hand. They believed it was their responsibility to ensure that all of their students graduate from high school. Responding to the first research question, they mentioned the importance of graduating more than twenty times.

Mr. Wade (Mariah Technical High School) explained that he calls down to his office "every kid . . . that's not passing everything at the end of the second quarter and [says], 'Hey, you're not on track to graduate. What's the plan here?'" He and Mrs. Michelle (Dennis Vocational High School) both track data to ensure that each student has all the credits necessary to graduate. With this established, they go on to focus on other factors.

For "Black males," Mr. Wade commented, the obstacle to graduation was most likely "an exam." Mrs. Michelle pointed out that the Regents exam, required by New York State, is the one "the kids have difficulty with." Accordingly, she targets students for work on the Regents and other specific stumbling blocks to graduation. All six principals said that they make it their business to know what their at-risk students need by looking at the data for each graduation requirement. The data tells them what to work on most intensively.

Mrs. Michelle spoke about using data to put in safety nets to catch students before they fall: "I think there's safety nets there that before we lose 'em, and they're too far behind, and you just get that feeling of, 'I'm never gonna be able to make this.' We will do some targeted AIS [academic intervention services] with students as well."

She also ensures that her school counselors and assistant principals "really take responsibility" for their students. "I have an assistant principal that meets a class when they are in tenth grade and stays with them," she explained. "And there are two counselors that are assigned to that grade as well, and we rotate off." By their senior year, every student, especially those most at risk, are well known to staff members "inside and out," she says. And so is the family. As Mr. Pierre of Dayton Central High School put it, relationship building with students is key. The "right adult at the right time allows us to tap into what we think is the single most crucial piece to getting kids to the finish line, that is at risk, and that is building quality relationships."

Mrs. Etchika (Duplessy-Johnson High School) employs a strategy "called 'Extended Class' that meets four times a week for an hour and a half. In that class . . . [an] advisor relationship is built, and it's sort of like a small family, within the family of this school." All of the principals found that keeping students on track required deliberately building relationships.

With respect to the *you've got to own it* subtheme of *keep everybody on track*, Mr. Wade put the ethos this way: "You're here and you're ours; we take responsibility for you and our number one goal is growth." The six successful principals were relentless in their conviction that principals must own their students' educational experience. As. Mrs. Michelle, said: "This is the direction we need to go, because we wanna get you across this stage."

"It's steady," Mrs. Johnson (Emanuel Honors High School) explained. "The expectations don't waiver. And [the students] know not to waiver with them. And it's somewhere that they want to be. They know that if they keep the course, . . . they're going to graduate. And we're going to do what we can [to help] by having the afterschool program." High school principals who achieve significant improvement in graduation rates all embrace the paradigm that every student in their schools belongs to them.

We care was the second theme that emerged in response to research question 1. Mrs. Etchika explained that her students, especially the Black males, "know that when they come here, the adults here care about them." The culture she leads is one in which teachers and administrators care about their students. "We focus largely on building relationships, and I think that makes a huge difference in how our students perform." She spoke of understanding that "if you don't get to a child's heart and mind and help them deal with whatever's going on in life, they're not gonna focus on the academics." Mr. Pierre (Dayton Central High School) added: "We spend a lot of time talking about things like accountability, and having a strong mindset, and how to build the relationships, and . . . having the courage to lead others."

Make school fun again was a subtheme of *we care*. Along with showing students that they care, principals spoke about the importance of inspiring them to *want* to be in school. "We value academics, we value the arts, we value athletics, and we value just the overall school culture and climate that we want . . . to be dynamic, vibrant, nurturing, supporting, challenging," Mr. Jordan (Mia Central High School) told me. He added: "I personally want kids to have fun in education. I think school should be fun." Mr. Pierre agreed: "You can either keep trying to give them more work, and more stuff to do, more assignments, and try to think that that's going to make them study harder and work more, or you know, you can kind of go backward, and just try to make school fun again, and make it so that they like it so much that they'd rather be here than not."

Both principals talked about running contests, pep rallies, and other engaging activities. Others mentioned clubs. "We're blessed with extracurricular activities," Mrs. Michelle commented. "We've got all kinds of clubs and activities. We say, 'If there is an interest and 10 kids, well, there could be a club here.'"

Diversity is celebrated, not just tolerated emerged as another *we care* subtheme. The principals were clear about their belief in the importance of diversity and in employing leadership strategies to support their beliefs. Mr. Jordan explained:

> I understand that the second an African American boy walks in the door of this school, he has a strong chance of not graduating if you follow the numbers. So, they're at risk just by being African American. My goal is to beat the odds, so we just pay extra attention to them and we put extra effort into creating things that speak to them.

Mrs. Michelle said that, in her school, diversity was "not tolerated. It's something that's . . . celebrated." She and the other principals implement and support African American History programs, targeted counseling interventions to assure Black males feel supported, and such activities as allowing students to speak to fellow students and to staff about their hijabs and cultural backgrounds.

The *student voice* subtheme of *we care* is related to the celebration of diversity. Mrs. Johnson told me that every student needs a voice: "I think it's so important that no matter where we are with our students, because we have so many diverse students that they all need a voice." Mr. Jordan spoke of nurturing their "creativity and entrepreneurial mindset." Mr. Pierre related how his school established a new student government "to try to provide authentic voice for the kids and make them feel engaged in what we're doing." The principals all believed that hearing the student's voice should be a part of their decision-making process. Furthermore, Mr. Jordan added, "it's a give and take where you're giving students opportunities to build their culture."

One of the biggest points every principal made was that nothing within a school is possible without teachers; therefore, *staff are valued* emerged as yet another subtheme of *we care*.

Mr. Jordan put it this way: "A school is not successful unless their faculty's moving forward and feeling supported." Mr. Wade explained that his school celebrates "a staff member of the month every month that we put out there on the wall. We do a PA announcement about them, which creates a little bit of competition, which is nice. We're always walking around thanking [the staff]." The principals were all anxious to ensure that the caring culture they wanted for students was also modeled for their teachers.

Clear discipline is the third major theme to emerge in response to the first research question. The principals agreed that if a school is going to be successful, every person in it must feel safe there. Clear discipline creates safer schools. Mrs. Michelle explained how important it is for students to know the expectations of discipline in her school:

> We do have expectations about what it means to be a citizen here in the building; a level of stability that we're going to conduct ourselves with. I mean, that's ultimately what our goal is. Everybody has the right to come to school here, and feel free from being afraid, or being bullied or harassed.

Yet every principal took a different approach to discipline. As Mr. Jordan put it, "We're going to be creative about the type of consequences you get." Nevertheless, two important goals were common to all: discipline should be restorative in nature, and academics were never lost as a focus in disciplining students.

"If we have to suspend you," Mr. Jordan said, "I am going to hire you a tutor and you better be there when he knocks on your door." He continued: "We've always supported the extra expense that comes with discipline. You want to run a safe school, but you're going to create a snowball effect if you don't have the educational components somehow rolling."

While each principal had their own disciplinary strategy, all believed restorative practices were the most effective approach to dealing with most negative behaviors. *Hug it out* was thus a subtheme of *clear discipline*. The principals interviewed believed that punitive measures, including suspensions, do not decrease negative student behaviors.

"We know that suspension really doesn't work," Mrs. Etchika flatly stated. Mrs. Michelle talked about avoiding highly punitive measures because of the impact these have on academics. "If you get in that discipline realm, things start to get close, because you might get behind in credits. . . . Ultimately, our goal is to keep everybody on track for graduation."

Although these principals were not big on punitive measures, they all insisted on the importance of holding students accountable for their actions. Mr. Wade admitted his initial hesitation over using restorative practices to enforce accountability. "I would be the first to admit I was kind of skeptical. We're all going to sit in a circle, we're going to hug it out, right?" After much PD and training, he said he came around, calling his original viewpoint "ignorant" and saying that learning about restorative practices was "for me . . . a real growth . . . I had a fixed mindset when I was introduced, watched it a little bit, developed a growth mindset, and now it's our assistant principals, that's their practice."

Other principals also talked about how they implemented restorative practices in their schools. Mrs. Etchika used peace circles, while Mrs. Michelle favored mediation and encouraged students to talk about their disagreements: "We do try to talk our way through and make sure that everybody's heard, and that there's understanding about whatever the offense was perceived, or real, and try to bring an end. We have done mediations that have involved whole families." The chief objective is to keep students in school and not suspended.

Research Question 2

For those strategies identified, how are they being implemented, and how might they be replicated in other schools?

In the analysis of the responses to this question and to the associated follow-up questions, two overarching themes emerged. The first is *really embracing that PD*, with subthemes *collaboration is a practice* and *we're always thanking them*. The second is *every student has someone*, together with the subtheme *we're taking you higher*.

Really embracing that PD, the first theme, is about the importance of using PD to increase graduation rates for Black males in your school. "It is important to make sure your staff has the professional development that is needed," Mrs. Johnson noted. Mr. Wade emphasized using university partnerships to increase cultural awareness. "We had NYU in here. We had a lot of services come into help us. And we got to this harmony where we are now of everyone gets along."

Collaboration is a practice emerged as a subtheme of *really embracing that PD*. In conjunction with PD, principals spoke about the importance of collaborating with teachers and valuing them as professionals. Mrs. Johnson explained how she collaborates with her teachers: "At the end of every marking period, I meet with my teachers. I call them in one by one, and we talk about where maybe they were successful. What can we do? How are we going to do that? And we make note of it to see who met their goal." Mrs. Etchika spoke about building into teacher schedules time for meetings. "We have time with our staff every Thursday to meet for 2 hours." She explained that they discuss specific students in their classes: "I'm seeing this, this, and this. That's a severe issue for him. What are you guys seeing?" They go on to consider what they can do, collectively, as the student's teacher, to help him or her succeed.

Mrs. Michelle explained how she uses data from collaborative meetings to increase student achievement:

> The teachers . . . review data, [and] they preview unit exams. Where did kids have difficulty last year? What can we do to pre-teach this to help kids be successful along the way? And then when they are finished, and if they give a unit assessment, they will review that data as well.

All the principals believed that student-teacher-administrator collaboration can be used to increase student graduation rates. They also believed that focusing on creating a positive culture for teachers is important. This is where the *we're always thanking them* subtheme of *really embracing that PD* comes in. Mr. Wade specifically discussed how he thanks teachers and does so with the specific objective of increasing graduation rates among his students. "If you want your kids to be successful, your teachers need to be successful. At the end of the day, [teachers are] going to affect [students] the most, not me." He explained that he was "always walking around thanking them. 'Thank you for what you do.' . . . I'll stop them [in the hall:] 'Hey, I just want to thank you.' One thing I learned here is that if you appreciate people, they're going to show up and work not for me, but for the kids."

The research demonstrates that school principals have a direct impact on teachers and an indirect impact on student achievement.[15] The principals interviewed believed that creating a culture of care for their teachers translates into a caring culture for students.

Every student has someone is the second major theme the responses to research question 2 surfaced. All the principals believed that, for students to achieve a high level of success, each must feel that they have someone who is *for* them, who's got their back. For their part, principals and teachers must believe that relationships with students really do matter.

Mrs. Etchika developed a strategy to provide each student with an advisor. "That goes back to . . . relationship building. Every advisor has about 18 students on average that they are responsible for. [Each student meets with their advisor] one-on-one . . . every other week. Every student has someone . . . they are communicating with about any and everything involving them."

Mr. Wade assigns every new student a teacher:

> When you come in [as a student] there's an entry . . . plan. So, if you registered here today, you would come in, you would meet with a guidance counselor, you would meet with one of the administrators, [and] you would have an ambassador to walk you around. For 5 weeks, you have a teacher [assigned, to whom] you report to that teacher at the end of every week.

Mrs. Johnson agreed that all students should have someone. Her approach is to assign peer tutors, not teachers, to students who are in need. "I found that students sometimes learn best from other students because . . . students sometimes can reach other students [in ways] that we just can't . . . so, I . . . implement[ed] a peer tutoring program. [After a year,] teachers are saying the results are pretty good. Kids are doing better."

We're taking you higher is a subtheme of *every student has someone*. In New York State, to graduate, students need a specific number of credits and a passing grade on "Regents exams." Mr. Wade said, "We started looking at the exams, and that's our focus because that's . . . been the biggest hurdle [for] Black males. If a Black male didn't graduate, it wasn't because he didn't have his 22½ credits [but] because [he] struggled with an exam." Mr. Wade emphasized pinpointing the problem that needed to be addressed:

> Maybe it's a deficiency in reading. What can we do to help you? Or maybe . . . we're going to put you in academic intervention services [AIS], so we're taking you out of an elective, we're taking you out of study hall, and we start pigeon-holing [you] to make sure [you are] prepared for that next assessment.

Mrs. Johnson talked about giving her students personal care time. This gives them permission to leave lunch to meet with a teacher for extra help in a class they are failing. "It's an hour every day instead of lunch. It's your time to go and work with your social studies teacher because you have work you need to make up."

Mrs. Michelle's students are on a block schedule, and she leaves 45 minutes at the end of the day for all teachers to be available:

> Teachers are all available, kids are all available, and they . . . can make appointments to see different teachers. Sometimes we place kids in particular study halls: "You're going with your math teacher three days a week, and you're going to go with your global teacher the other three days of the cycle." We will do some targeted AIS with students as well. If they haven't been successful, we [also] do a test-prep block for them.

The six principals had a wide variety of strategies intended to ensure that students, including Black males, would graduate. Varied as the approaches were, all were strategically based on data.

Research Question 3

What, if any, aspects of culturally proficient leadership are being employed by successful principals?

Upon analysis, three themes emerged from the answers prompted by Question 3 and follow-ups. The first theme was *adapt to diversity*. This in turn suggested the subthemes *they're all our kids* and *it's just what we do*. The second theme was *value diversity*, and the third, *manage the dynamics of difference*, which suggested one subtheme, *courageous conversations*. All of these themes and subthemes relate to culturally proficient leadership, a mindset common to all six principals, and they are key elements of showing students love, which was discussed in *What We Mean By "Love,"* at the very beginning of this chapter. This discussion will not be repeated here, but it is necessary to discuss the need to have *courageous conversations* with those whose culture differs from that of Black students.

Culturally proficient leadership manages the dynamics of difference when people of one culture interact with those of other cultures. Mrs. Etchika described what she encounters when some teachers resist cultural changes in her school.

Some "come to me and say, 'I don't understand why I have to go' to workshops or PD for help with cross-cultural communication. And they don't understand," Mrs. Etchika explained. "Students know who those teachers are. They know who they are, I know who they are, because we can watch the way that they treat students." Mrs. Etchika sends even these resisters teachers for training, explaining to them that she has seen the trouble they have communicating cross-culturally.

Similarly, Mr. Wade recalled the conversations he has when cultural conflicts arise between students and teachers: "Where we have a conflict with the staff and a student, and not racial conflict, I call it an 'understanding conflict' . . . . When [such] a conflict happens, it's [usually] because we have staff members [who are] relatively new" to the school. To manage such instances of the dynamics of difference, Mr. Wade said he has "an honest conversation with the teacher. So, there's two things I go with here. I call them honest conversations, and I [also] call them *three people in a room.* . . . [because it's as if] you're [suddenly] in the mix of two stories that don't add up. Somebody's bending the truth."

Mr. Wade even attempts to manage the dynamics of difference within the community:

> When I go out in the community, "Oh you're the principal [of that] school? [That school has] changed [a lot,] so [now it's a] tough place." And the first word out of my mouth, I say, "Why, because we've got Black kids? Not many kids get removed for disrespect to a staff member. Come check it out because it's *not* 'a tough place.' And by the way, yeah, you're right, we do have Black kids, but they're not bad kids."

Mr. Wade was adamant about defending his students of color, not only in the school but out in the community. *That* is a courageous conversation. To paraphrase the Gospel, Greater love hath no man than this—to speak courageously the truth he knows firsthand about the young Black males he educates, respects, appreciates, and is determined to stand up for.

Chapter 2

Some Do Overcome

The transition from elementary school or middle school to high school has always presented challenges. There is a disconnect between eighth grade and ninth, as students are suddenly required to work more independently. There is less teacher supervision and more autonomy. For many students, regardless of race or ethnicity, it's like getting tossed into the deep end of the pool.

In 2003, Melissa Roderick, a University of Chicago specialist in urban school reform, wrote an article published in *Urban Education*. "What's Happening to the Boys?" was the title and "Early High School Experiences and Outcomes among African American Male Adolescents in Chicago" was the subtitle.[1] The study revealed a decline in academic motivation and student engagement, especially among Black males. Roderick's data demonstrate that Black males do, on average, struggle in secondary schools.

Most educators believe that, by age thirteen, students should be capable of working with very little guidance and supervision. The problem is that Black males typically enter secondary schools at a significantly lower academic level than peers of other racial and ethnic backgrounds. Stress this reality by suddenly increasing academic autonomy and decreasing teacher oversight, and you have a recipe for academic failure.

But it gets even worse.

HOSTILITY, RACIAL STEREOTYPING,
AND MYTHOLOGY

Black males entering secondary schools are faced with adult hostility, which creates a negative environment in which they become disengaged from the school. The disengagement only widens the achievement gap between White and Black males in test scores and graduation rates.[2] In fact, more than 40 percent of Black males in this country will not graduate from high school. Black males drop out of high school at a rate of 10.6 percent as compared to their White classmates' rate of 6.3 percent. One study has shown that Black males in high schools internalize racial stereotypes that hobble them academically. Such internalization is a predictor of self-handicapping behaviors in Black male high school students, and the behaviors contribute to the high dropout rates in this group.[3]

Evidence based on studies of Black males who attended urban schools and were subsequently incarcerated reveals how their school experience contributed to the school-to-prison pipeline. These students are often placed in remedial classes, which make them feel incapable of achieving academic success. Due in part to the high rates of suspension of Black males, they are made to feel like the outright enemies of education. Those who dropped out and later ended up behind bars felt frustrated with the educational process. They believed teachers were predictors of their academic success, and they felt more valued in lower grades and less valued through middle school and high school.[4]

Several myths have developed concerning Black males in schools. Among these is the myth of parental noninvolvement. Many educators believe that if these students benefitted from greater parental involvement in their lives, they would be successful. Yet a great deal of ambiguity surrounds the precise meaning of parental "involvement" or "support." A 2010 study analyzed the thoughts and perceptions teachers and administrators had about the Black males in their school. Teachers in particular asked for more parental involvement but could not articulate how this would assist them in increasing student achievement.[5] Another myth is that Black males fail academically because of lack of motivation. This is related to the hoary stereotype that Black males are inherently and incorrigibly lazy. Relying on such frankly racist stereotypes is a common practice among adults who fail to build relationships with their students.[6]

The achievement gap between Black and White students may contribute to a hostile culture within the school, which promotes additional negative stereotypes about Black males and their families. For students of color, underachievement can become normalized and expected as educators and others accept low performance as the by-product of factors beyond their control.

A 2008 analysis of two suburban school districts investigated why some districts were experiencing success in closing the achievement gap while others were not. Those schools unable to close the gap embraced two myths: first, that Black males have parents who do not care for them and, second, that socioeconomic status is a predictor of academic success. This second argument does have some merit, but it is also true that countless impoverished Black males do graduate from high school.[7]

Another corrosive stereotype is that the academic failure of Black males is a product of their culture, which, some believe, does not support hard work or the value of education. In these ways, some people, educators included, attempt to normalize the long-standing achievement gap by coming up with stereotyped rationales.

These myths have one bottom line in common. They blame racial achievement gap on the students, their families, and Black culture—everything except ineffective teaching methods and lack of administrative leadership. With the blame shifted, schools do not focus on closing the achievement gap, a problem they see as beyond their power to solve or even ameliorate.[8]

THE SELF-FULFILLING PROPHECY OF FAILURE

When Black students, especially male students, enter our schools, their teachers and administrators treat them differently from other students. The difference only increases after the transition to high school. They are suspended at disproportionate rates, and they are expelled because of zero-tolerance policies enacted by administrators who believe that mandatory expulsion promotes safer schools.[9]

A recent quantitative research study of Chicago Public Schools discovered that for an urban school to *appear* successful, the school must feel and seem safe to those in the building. To create safety—or, really, the appearance of safety—administrators may use punitive measures rather than proactive or restorative strategies to discipline bad behavior by Black male students.

Thus, these students are routinely not viewed as equal members of the school community. The data demonstrates that 50 percent of Black males in grades 6 through 12 had been suspended, compared to just 21 percent of White males. In addition, 17 percent of Black males had been expelled from school compared to only 1 percent of White males.[10]

Another study from 2010 explored the results of Black male overrepresentation in exclusionary disciplinary practices, such as suspension, in-school suspension (ISS), and expulsion. When students are suspended at a high rate, they inevitably become disengaged from the school community. Black males forced out of the school through suspension have the lowest academic success, which anyone with common sense must associate with poor attendance. Moreover, they feel alienated and, therefore, often attempt to find "success" in other areas—typically involving illicit activity. Their exclusion-induced alienation is associated with the creation of a school-to-prison pipeline.

As students are repeatedly suspended, they are made to feel like outcasts for the simple reason that they are cast out. Those who run the school are sending them a powerful message: *School is not for you. You do not belong here.* It is not just that they are being denied an education, which so essential to laying claim on any viable future, they are being banished from school, which is often their only safe haven from the mean streets. The system is creating outcasts, victims, and criminals because we who run the system do not accept—or do not know how to accept—Black males for who they are.

Nor are they merely cast out. Often, adding insult to their injury, many times students who have committed an offense are arrested at school—a tactic that adds public shaming to their punishment. Without doubt, bad behavior calls for a response, but the objective of the justice system should be correction, not humiliation and rejection. Too often lacking in the criminal justice system, humanity should be practiced in abundance in our schools. Black males are three times more likely to be incarcerated than any other race. While they make up 12.4 percent of the U.S. population, they account for more than 35 percent of the prison population. Black males thirty or younger have a 52 percent chance of being jailed.

There are three top contributing reasons for the incarceration of young men of color. One is behavior, aspects of which may be correlated with school, but the other two are related directly to school: academic problems and academic disengagement.[11] Fail in school—or have school fail you—and there is a good chance that you end up behind bars.

LIVED EXPERIENCES OF BLACK MALES IN HIGH SCHOOL

We live up or we live down to what the world expects from us. The painfully telling thing about the experience of Black males in high school is that it is far easier to find their incarceration rate than their graduation rate.[12] Nevertheless, while the majority do lag in many content areas, a significant number excel in such key content areas as math and science. These high achievers have four universally recognized themes in common: positive teacher influence, positive peer influence, success in sports, and belief in economic mobility.

We should consider adding a fifth theme. High achievers are exposed to models of leadership in their schools, both through strong, caring teachers and strong, caring administrators.

Without doubt, some Black males do have a positive experience in urban schools and do have teachers who consistently encourage them academically. One high-achieving student reported that his teacher challenged him to achieve nothing less than scores of 100 percent in math. He believes that, because of this encouragement, he made that goal, and he graduated. Teacher motivation and high expectations transformed and enabled these students to believe they could earn high academic grades. Moreover, one of the most persistent myths of Black performance in school, parental involvement, has been found to play virtually no role in the success of the high achievers.[13]

In contrast to high achievers encouraged to aim high, most Black male students experience low expectation from their teachers. Students dread coming to class when their teachers have such low expectations for them. The message of these low expectations is that the teachers are not interested in them. Yet it is imperative that Black male students feel that they belong in the school they attend and that their teachers do care about them and want them to succeed.[14] Moreover, many Black male students attend secondary schools that offer little or no exposure to advanced placement (AP) classes and higher-level sciences. Indeed, they have severely limited exposure to science fairs and college preparatory classes.[15]

It is no wonder that these students feel uncared for and uncared about. Believing that they do not belong, they find themselves facing a seemingly insuperable barrier to academic success. By failing to offer AP classes, failing to encourage them to take the AP classes that are offered, or even actively discouraging them from attempting these classes, schools create self-fulfilling prophecies of failure. In this, they may claim to be realistic. But it is a reality of their own creation.[16]

BLACK MALES CAN EXCEL

As steeply as the odds are stacked against them, Black males can and do achieve academic success. To date, there are over one million Black men in college. Each one of them is there because he received the support of a principal. Secondary school principals in such states as New Jersey achieve a 70 percent graduation rate for their Black male students. Yet most principals elsewhere across the country have a difficult time increasing the achievement rates among these students.[17]

How Do Male Students of Color Beat the Odds?

Those students who overcome the odds and the obstacles, graduating at the top of their classes, have chosen either to ignore the negative stereotypes or deliberately prove them wrong by excelling academically. Nevertheless, these choices come at a psychological cost. High-performing students report feeling "pressured to continually prove their intellectual worth to their teachers."[18]

Other strategies high-achieving Black male students employ include trying to be seen as satisfactory in the eyes of their teachers by smiling often, appearing friendly, hanging with smart kids, and dressing in preppy styles. They are, in fact, desperate to fit in.[19] And yet, as a 2016 study of seven midwestern schools shows, the number of Black male students in special education is disproportionately high. Often, the reason students are sent to special ed is misbehavior.

Black males are referred to special education classes at a rate three times higher than that of any other population. One study quotes a special education teacher: "Whenever we are having chronic behavior problems, it is a little Black boy. We call them the 'Duwans,'" a name the special education coordinator at this teacher's school used for Black males who are referred to special education by teachers who describe them as "emotionally disturbed," "developmentally disabled," or even "mentally retarded." The underlying complaint, however, is typically "behavior problems," disruptive to the class, and which the referring teachers generally ascribe to poverty, as if to rationalize their referrals by citing a circumstance beyond their control or accountability.[20]

Reversing the Trend

Undoing myths and stereotypes requires leadership, and while it is true that teachers must be prepared to expect more of their Black male students—and perhaps more from their students in general—the transformation has to take place not just between one student and one teacher and not just within one classroom, but across the entire building. Creating transformation on this level calls for the leadership of principals.

A 2012 survey of five reputable principal leadership programs across the nation provided a measure of what can be done to grow and develop the real-world skillset of principals. The authors of the survey concluded that successful principal leadership preparation programs should:

1. Have a clear focus on standards-based curriculum.
2. Include field-based internships, cohort groups, active instructional strategies, rigorous recruitment, and strong partnerships with schools and districts to support high-quality field experiences.[21]

Good principal preparation programs need to train administrators for the rigors of working in an urban school. The dismal graduation rates among many Black male students demonstrate this need. Principals who complete their training should be able to:

1. Establish a culture that fosters a positive environment for teaching and learning.
2. Promote professional collaboration.
3. Promote the instructional abilities and PD of teachers.

4. Marshal resources and systems toward the development of teaching and learning.
5. Enlist the support of the community and parents.

While there is evidence that parental involvement in their child's education does *not* play a pivotal role, it is also apparent that the best preparation programs train principals to own their data and to include parents as well as the community in instruction. Schools that manage to implement these requirements succeed in raising graduation rates. Those that are not data-driven and do not reach out to parents and community make little impact on graduation rates. Principals in these schools tend not to understand the value of parents, and they simply blame students, parents, and the community at large—anything and everything outside of the building—for their students' failure to graduate.[22]

Unfortunately, most principals are not yet being properly trained to enter the field of administration in an urban setting. That is, they are being trained to manage the day-to-day operation of schools, but not to lead the destiny of the school, to create a vision, to ask questions about good instruction and curriculum, and, in particular, to lead urban schools. They are trained to be managers in a situation where CEOs are needed.

This is an acute deficiency, because research clearly demonstrates that principals matter. They are in position to make a difference, provided they are properly prepared to do so. The national crisis of depressed graduation rates among Black males is linked arm in arm with the shortage of properly trained principals and programs to train them.[23]

PRINCIPALS NEED HELP

For at least fifty years, accountability has been a constant refrain in education, with administrators pushed to demonstrate their ability to increase student achievement with such federal initiatives as No Child Left Behind, Race to the Top, and the Every Student Succeeds Act. Today, principals are required to attend training programs that prepare them to meet expectations.

They need all the help they can get to develop necessary leadership skills. Colleges must also recruit high-quality aspiring principals to enroll in their training programs. Principals must be afforded the best opportunities to succeed. Researchers have produced a list of five transformational leadership practices principals should master:

1. Inspiring a shared vision
2. Modeling the way
3. Challenging the process
4. Enabling others to act
5. Encouraging the heart

Of these, the two practices that have had the greatest positive impact on student achievement have been shown to be #1 and #3, inspiring a shared vision and challenging the process. The researchers recommend that principals improve in all levels of leadership, but especially in inspiring a shared vision and challenging the process.[24]

Over the past decade, traditional educational preparation programs have failed to prepare school principals as leaders by failing to connect theoretical concepts with practical application. Scholars in the field believe that there is a disconnect between what principals must do on a day-to-day basis versus what they are taught to do in college classrooms.[25]

We have already seen that principals have an indirect impact on student achievement, but they need training, instruction, and support to lead their buildings in ways that positively impact graduation rates, especially among young males of color. Currently, they are shouldering the brunt of the national demand for accountability after fifty years of well-meaning legislative initiatives have all proved costly failures. Neither legislators nor teachers have succeeded in significantly improving graduation rates among Black males. Billions of dollars have been thrown at the problem—to no avail. Principals are the last men and women standing. It is up to them.

We have also seen that, while Black males have the lowest graduation rates among any population in the country, graduating from high school at the rate of 59 percent, many do succeed and are, in fact, high performers. New Jersey (among some other states) graduates 70 percent of their Black male high school students. Some two million Black men hold college degrees today, and, right now, more than a million young Black males are in college. As for my own school, McKinley High, the four-year graduation rate for Black males is now 93 percent.

Underprepared as they are, principals nevertheless find themselves the front line in the fight to lift Black male graduation rates. Those who study education are in agreement. There is a need for secondary school principals to acquire more strategies for increasing these dismal graduation rates. Armed with such knowledge, they are in position to lead teachers, students, and families toward higher achievement and greater academic success.

The next chapter, Ten Steps Forward, introduces part II of this book, introducing the ten-step program instituted at McKinley High School, which dramatically improved graduation rates among our Black male students.

Will these ten steps make up for fifty years of failed initiatives? To a remarkable degree, they do.

Do they supply everything our beleaguered principals need to lead the necessary improvement? Well, they are an excellent beginning.

More important, the ten-step program demonstrates that graduation rates can be raised. Moreover, even under the worst, most discouraging conditions, a significant number of Black male students do overcome the odds against them. They achieve. And they don't just get by. They achieve at high levels.

Facing us, then, is not an impossible dream. It is an achievement gap between one cohort and another. It is a gap that can be narrowed. And even closed.

Chapter 3

Ten Steps Forward

The preface and first two chapters of this book are all about a journey. The destination is a chance at a longer life and a better life. As I learned early in my own life, young Black men who do not graduate from high school too often pass through prison and too often die young and violently. Human behavior is complex, but certain cause-and-effect relationships that impact that behavior are shockingly simple, reducible to some vital data and a few *if-then* statements.

We know that the numerical data reveals a huge gap between White high school graduation rates and those for young Black males. The data also reveals a great disparity between the fate of young Black males who fail to graduate versus those who do. Crunch the numbers even a little bit, and you come out with this: *If* a Black male does not finish high school, *then* he has a high probability of a short, violent life, which often includes prison. *If* a Black male does graduate, *then* all the achievement gaps between him and his White counterparts narrow and even close as life opens up, stretching out into a long future of real possibility.

This is a book about transforming the first *if-then* into the second. What the nongraduation versus graduation data reveals is the power of understanding and love. Understanding begins with the data, which shows us what each student needs to move the needle from failure in a range of academic subjects to success and, consequently, from failing to graduate to graduating. For many Black male students, it is the difference between death and life.

Once we understand the data, we understand how to help. But the desire and the drive to help come from love. All of us whose work is educating children need to love the children we educate. That means honoring their diversity. That means leaving no child out, pushing no child away. The kids in your school building? They are *your* kids, all of them. You need a big heart to take them all on, but let me tell you, it is a lot easier to honor, love, and include your students than it is to bear within you the burden of baseless assumptions, inherent biases, bitterness, cynicism, contempt, and, yes, even fear. Unsurprisingly, these attitudes discourage children from achieving excellence in school. Perhaps more surprisingly, the same attitudes discourage the teachers, administrators, and parents from giving vulnerable male students of color all that they need.

We are all wondrously complex beings, but, ultimately, we all have the same basic needs. We need to be understood. We need to be respected. We need to be loved. Sooner or later, we also all need to be helped, to be lifted up. The right data enables us to understand what to do to help. The love will drive the will to mobilize and apply that understanding.

Chapter 2 zoomed in on schools that achieve Black male graduation rates of 70 percent and higher, sometimes much higher. It highlights the successes that have emerged and that continue to emerge out of the long, dreary narrative of national failure. That chapter is about the exhilarating, liberating things that happen when we succeed in reversing our expectations of failure. It is a glimpse into the educational mindset capable of driving a venture into success.

The opening of this book is a journey toward the willingness to embrace the power and potential of diversity, to proclaim of every student in the building, "They're all our kids," and to motivate every student, teacher, and administrator to aim higher.

Research shows that teachers and, especially, principals *can* lead their schools away from the middle of the road. To do this, they must look away from the middle and up higher to find the outliers: the students, especially the Black males, who confound expectation and travel way off the middle of the road. A principal has the opportunity to lead everyone in the school to look to the extreme performers and dare to use *them* as examples for orchestrating success in that building.

Part II, the next part of this book, enumerates ten steps through which principals must lead their schools. They must, as it were, lead from the balcony, holding teachers accountable even as they simultaneously empower them to engage their students as what they truly are: stakeholders in their own success.

Part II explains each of the ten steps that my school, McKinley High School, Buffalo, New York, took to close the gap between Black male graduation rates and those of every other group. In seminars, podcasts, blogs, forums, articles, and other programs, I have brought these steps to other educators in New York State and elsewhere. Principals everywhere are now closing the gap, one school building at a time, throughout the United States. Leadership from the balcony looks out not only at your own school but across the nation. The victory in this campaign must be national, even global. But it must be won one building at a time, each day, semester, and year, over and over again.

THE STEPS

Step One: Data Dominates

Data and love are the drivers of success in increasing academic performance and closing the graduation gap. Step One is about tracking and understanding your data and knowing precisely what data you need to know: Black male referral and suspension rates; Black male state exam performance; Black male student attendance; Black male course passing, expulsions, student return rates, teacher attendance; and, of course, the Black male graduation rate in your school. In this step, you will learn what data to monitor at five- and ten-week intervals and how to recognize and act upon the warning signs at three and seven weeks.

You will find here a discussion of monitoring cohort data, of discovering who is ready to graduate, who still needs exams or courses for graduation, and who is substantially not ready to graduate. You will discover how to bring quantifiable data discipline to the monitoring of behavior by measuring the rate of incidents off school grounds and on school grounds as well as the change (+ or −) in short-term and long-term suspensions. Such data is used to support a range of positive disciplinary practices, including restorative justice, restorative discipline, in-school counseling, and incentive systems.

You also need to track more than student data. Teachers as well kids must be held accountable, so you must track teacher absences with academic performance.

Step Two: Goals? Make Them Realistically High

The second of the ten steps is setting realistically high goals. It is important to give equal weight to both the adverb and the adjective: "realistically" *and* "high." Another thing you will learn in taking this step is that setting goals—clearly articulated, concrete goals—is essential. Vague aspirations, hopes, and theoretical abstractions will not help you to motivate improved performance. Finally, the goals must be applied throughout the school.

In this step, you will find a discussion about ensuring that goals are lofty but realistic. This need not be a matter of opinion. You will learn here how to derive current goals from historical facts, that is, the data of previous years. You need goals for every academic area within your building. Everybody—you, students, and teachers—need to talk about the goals. Do so at every staff meeting, faculty meeting, and in every one-on-one conversation, and in every class.

Each goal must be capable of quantitative assessment. Like the goals in football, soccer, or hockey, the goals you and other school stakeholders set are ways of keeping score and comparing scores over time. This way, everyone will know where the school is headed. No hunches, intuitions, guesses, or opinions are required when you have data. Based on previous performance as measured by percentage of goals achieved, figure out next year's goals. Keep a close eye on passing goals, which are second in importance only to the goals you set for graduation rates.

Step Three: If You Don't Like What's Being Said, Change the Conversation

Step Three is about taking control of the narrative—of what's being said about your school. When we at McKinley High got tired of being dismissed as a "middle-of-the-road" school, we decided to call *ourselves* "The Best School in the Land." That forced us to work toward changing our narrative to live up to the label. In this way, we set a goal of bringing reality into line with aspiration. (It worked!)

Step Four: Hold Teachers Accountable

Step Four on the path to improving graduation rates calls for principals and other administrators to build strong, 100 percent accountable relationships with teachers by making every teacher responsible for hitting all student learning objectives and all the school's goals. Led by the principal, every administrator in the building must thank and celebrate every teacher in the building. When needed, however, frank and courageous corrective conversations must also be had. Base all criticism—and all praise—on data. Mobilize data to drive improvement. Make everything important by measuring every important thing.

Step Five: Resources—Prioritize, Focus, Allocate

As the orchestrator of success, the principal must lead this step, which calls for prioritizing, focusing, and allocating the school's resources. Direct those resources to academics and other enunciated goals. Reiterate and prioritize the main goal—graduation—which is the goal toward which everything else must contribute.

This step calls for some creative action. Engage in partnerships with colleges. Create free tutoring programs and encourage teacher tutors to push in proactively. Do not neglect peer-to-peer tutoring programs.

Principals and other leaders must be highly intentional when it comes to the allocation of resources, which includes issues of staffing. The best teachers should be deployed where they are needed the most. Vacancies in the teaching staff must be filled promptly. Ensure that teachers know they have a duty to hold conversations with students and with each other one-on-one and that they also must plan together.

Step Six: Discover Their Big Why

This step is very consequential. You need to create space for Black males to discover their "Big Why." You cannot succeed in any enterprise if you do not know *why* you are even trying.

In the case of McKinley High, we found our collective Big Why in the fact that we are the largest career technical education school in Buffalo. We leveraged this to help each student discover his or her Big Why. We offer our students knowledge that will enable them to literally build a house from the ground up. They can learn plumbing, electrical, HVAC, print media, horticulture, and aquatic ecology. They can even attend an Urban Teacher Academy Program. They are provided multiple opportunities to discover that they can excel at something more than football or basketball.

The power of the Big Why is in demonstrating a connection between school curriculum and the "real world," which, after all, is where everyone's "Big Why" lives.

Step Seven: Work, Workout, Rest, Smile, Laugh, Hug Your Family, Keep Your Mind and Body Healthy

Step Seven is to get yourself healthy in mind and body and stay that way. Go to the gym, get adequate rest, eat well, find time to fully disengage from the hard work of saving lives. Spend time with your family. Take time off when you need it most. And make it your business to find many occasions to smile and laugh at work every single day. Working to improve student performance and your performance is some of the hardest work you can possibly find.

Step Eight: Red, Yellow, Green—Target Student Intervention

Data is *not* about anonymity or uniformity. The eighth step is targeted student intervention, indicating, student by individual student, just what kinds of intervention may be necessary to ensure graduation. For high-performing students, rigor is increased. For others, you need to craft strategically customized testing strategies and graduation conversations. In this step, teacher mentors are deployed. Raise graduation levels by any means necessary. At McKinley, we introduced an innovative night school program.

Step Nine: Reimagine Discipline

In our schools, as in our society, discipline is in dire need of more than reform. It requires reimagining. Suspension, which is the traditional big stick of academic discipline, is not just ineffective, it is stupidly destructive. The very last thing an underperforming student needs is to be forcibly disengaged from academics. All students need to be in their classes, and underperforming students need this most of all.

Step Nine calls for everyone in the building to put their minds and imaginations to work in crafting restorative disciplinary practices. This begins with reviewing the list of offenses. Is every so-called offense truly a violation? School, like society, needs good laws—but as few as possible. Love is the key. It is the first resort, as well as the last.

Step Ten: Celebrate . . . Everything!

The final step is to celebrate. More accurately, it is to make school itself a celebration. Find reasons to celebrate—just about everything. At McKinley, we have Shout-out Thursdays, and we name a Teacher of the Month every month. We recognize every student's achievement. Our goal is to let no good thing escape public notice. Instead of looking for the bad, we try to ensure that people notice the good and, having noticed it, make a very big deal about it.

Part II

THE TEN STEPS

Chapter 4

Step One

Data Dominates

We often hear that Americans don't "respect" teachers, that teaching is not a highly respected profession. Tell somebody you are an educator, and the response comes back like a kneejerk: "You know, we Americans just don't respect our teachers the way we should."

Next time you hear this, maybe you should ask, "On what data do you base that?"

Or maybe not. After all, such remarks are meant as a sort of empathetic complement, and maybe it would be mean spirited to challenge them.

Yet the truth is that there is no body of data to back up that claim. *Americans don't respect teachers?* This is an assumption well-meaning folks make without bothering to determine whether it is true or not.

There actually is data, a global study published by the Varkey Foundation in 2018.[1] Globally, on a list of fourteen professions, teachers are ranked, in terms of respect for the profession, tenth (primary teachers) and eleventh (secondary teachers), above web designers, social workers, and librarians. Interestingly, principals ("school leaders" or "head teacher") rank fourth, behind doctors, lawyers, and engineers.

So, an argument can be made that the people who say teachers are not respected are backed by the data. Yet the relatively high ranking of principals on the spectrum of respect does not support the idea that "educators" get little respect. One would think that the two professions—teacher and principal—would track more closely with one another, since both are educators.

Could it be that people respect principals because they are perceived as executives or bosses, whereas teachers are seen as the relatively low-paid rank and file?

Perhaps! But the truth is that some teachers perform so well that they deserve our highest respect and gratitude, while some perform at a much lower level, one that merits not praise but professional intervention and support to improve performance. If such a teacher still cannot produce excellent results, the low ranking, in terms of respect, is deserved. Conversely, only high-performing principals deserve to rank high in respect. The others are just getting free ride.

This is not an unfeeling position to take, because judging an educator's performance, whether a teacher or a principal, does not have to be a mere matter of subjective opinion. We have the data. Or we can get it.

But as it stands now, most parents, kids, and even administrators do not evaluate teachers on the basis of a quantifiable metric. Instead, we tend to get emotional impressions. Most students actually look up to their teachers. Or, at least, they really want to. Most adults think of the profession of teaching in idealistic, almost romanticized terms. Teachers are "dedicated" and "selfless," and the best of them have a "rare talent" and a "real love" for their "kids."

In some cases, these subjective impressions are accurate, but we cannot rely solely on subjective impressions. We need data. Data measures performance, provides benchmarks, highlights goals, and guides improvement.

No doubt, we witness bona fide magic when a teacher connects with a student, when a stubborn concept finally gets through to a kid or, even more, when a student gets really worked up about an idea or breaks through to the solution of a tough precalculus problem. But while we can take joy in the magic, we cannot depend on the magic. As the celebrated management guru W. Edwards Deming famously put it, "In God we trust. All others must bring data."

Step One, therefore, is all about the dominance of data, beginning with the four most important datapoints of all:

- Black males graduate from high school at the rate of 59 percent. This is the lowest among any population in the United States.
- Black males are suspended and referred to special education classes at rates

three times higher than any other population.

- Black males make up about 6 percent of the U.S. population but represent about 32 percent of the prison population.
- Males of all races and ethnicities who leave high school without a diploma have a mortality rate between ages thirty-nine and forty-six over twice that of high school graduates. Male Black high school dropouts in this same age group have the highest death rate of all: 11.6 percent, compared to 7.8 percent for Black males with a diploma.[2]

While these are the most urgent datapoints we need to know, here are four more to keep in mind. They tell the "other" truth about Black male performance in high school:

- Black males in some states graduate at the rate of 70 percent.
- More than two million Black males have college degrees.
- More than one million Black males are in college today.
- At McKinley High, in Buffalo, New York, the four-year graduation rate for Black males was 84 percent in 2019, and the five-year rate, 90 percent.

In 2020, my total graduation rate for all students was 87 percent, the highest in the decade, and a four-year grade rate for Black males at 93 percent. Here is why those first four datapoints are the most urgent. Regardless of race, gender, or ethnicity, students who do not graduate from high school have harder, more limited, and more dangerous lives, on average and by the numbers, than students who do graduate. It so happens that Black male students not only fall short of graduation at a much higher rate than those of any other race, ethnicity, or gender, but they also suffer more for it. More of them die, often violently, at a young age, and more of them spend some portion of their lives behind bars.

What do we do with this terrible reality?

As an educator, *use* it to elevate the goal of increasing the rates of graduation—for everyone, but especially for Black males—as the highest and most urgent priority. Do this, and you find yourself in some interesting conversations.

Ask a principal or superintendent this question: *Do you know your data?*

You may be met with silent incomprehension, or something like this: "Hell, yes, we know our data! Our graduation rate is blah blah blah, and we have X number of students, Y percent of whom are on free and reduced lunch. See? Like I said, we *do* know our data."

Offer thanks for the response, but understand that this level of academic bookkeeping is not sufficient.

We all need to collect more data and ask more questions about that data. Principals, teachers, superintendents, and parents must understand that data tells a story. We don't know what that story is going to be, but we do know that the more data we have, the clearer the message of that story, whatever it is, will be.

Here is a conversation I had not at all that long ago with the data guru in my school district.

"I'm looking at your data," she said, "and it is very confusing."

I know my eyebrows went up several inches.

"No, look," she went on. "Your data is *so* interesting. Your graduation rate far exceeds the rest of the district, and the number of students passing courses is greater than the rest of the district, but the level by which your kids pass is *lower* than the district average."

"Yes, I agree," I said. Then I waited for her to say something.

"I am confused by that," she finally said.

"But it makes sense."

She raised her hand to her forehead. "Please explain."

"Okay. Now this may sound wrong to you but hear me out. My goal is to get kids to graduate from high school. I whole-heartedly disagree with the proposition that testing is a measure of intelligence, especially when most research, for years now, is telling us that tests are not predictors of school success. So, I'm not all that interested in how well students did on any particular test or set of tests. I am far more concerned that they do well in the class and that they pass tests so that they can earn a high school diploma. For me, the significance of any test is strictly binary, 1 or 0, pass or fail, graduate or don't graduate."

This explanation did not completely satisfy her, and we agreed to disagree—philosophically, as educators. To be sure, there is room for philosophical debate, but a principal's job is better described as a *leader*, not an *educator*, and, given the performance crisis among Black male students, the only valid *leadership* philosophy is the one that prioritizes graduation above all else. To achieve this priority, all that matters is passing the test. It's like running for elected office. Election Day is the test. Yes, it's nice to win by a large margin, but if your objective is to be the mayor or senator or president, all that finally counts is making a fraction more than 50 percent. With a test at McKinley High School, that marker is a grade of 65. Do better than that, then God bless you. But at 65 you are already blessed.

As a leader, getting your students from 0 to 1 should be your highest priority. If it is the only metric by which graduation is achieved or not, then it is the primary metric by which principals should measure their performance as leaders.

SO, DO YOU KNOW YOUR DATA?

Ask principals and superintendents if they know their data, and they will likely answer in the affirmative and, by way of proof, tell you their graduation rate data.

Good! This is the most salient item to lead with. But it needs to be followed up with more.

As a leader in your school, you want to collect and analyze data that asks and answers the following:

- What is our attendance data, broken down into month by grade level?
- What is our test score data?
- What is our Regents score data? (Or data on any other final tests required for graduation.)
- What is our Black male formative assessment data?
- What is our course-passing data for Black males?
- What is our referral data for Black males?
- What is our suspension data—for Black males compared to other students within the school?

Then add these items:

- What is our *teacher* attendance data?
- What is our teachers' five-week course data for Black males and all students?
- What percentage of our teachers make phone calls home?

- How many calls do they make?
- What is our attendance data for the school's admin team?

Diversity data is key to developing cultural competence and fluency. Ask:

- What is our diversity data?
- How many Black males do we have in our school?
- What is the diversity data for our staff?
- How many students are on free and reduced-cost lunch programs?
- Do we know our social worker and school counseling data?
- How often do social workers and/or school counselors meet with students?
- What interventions do they make and how frequently for each?

Does this seem overwhelming? It should not be, yet the fact that few school leaders, especially those who are dissatisfied with the graduation rates in their school, ask, let alone answer, most of these questions. Most of them do not even know how to obtain the necessary data.

Yet every data category just mentioned directly impacts graduation rates, especially the rates of Black male students. Wandering in a data desert, no wonder so many administrators and teachers "lead" their students over a cliff instead of into a cap and gown. If we don't know what's happening or why or where it's taking our students, we cannot possibly know what to do.

No wonder the one piece of data most principals and superintendents do have at the tips of their fingers and the tops of their minds, graduation rates, is so intractably dismal, especially for Black males.

And, yes, this is a lot of data, and it can be a real pain to gather. But principals must see the numbers. It provides an objective picture that is at once individual yet that encompasses the whole building. Seeing the numbers allows principals, who are running a complex system, with multiple teachers teaching multiple subjects, to stay at 30,000 feet but still monitor students and teachers.

A Teacher's Data

Maybe the volume and range of data just reeled off is daunting. It will take some time, effort, and organizing to begin acquiring this information, but you can more immediately assess what kind of learning is taking place within a given classroom just by looking at the data of that particular teacher.

Start by looking at a teacher's course-passing data—essentially, how many students are passing her class. One teacher may have 60 percent of her students passing. Out of that 60 percent, say 48 percent score 65–69, the other 12 percent score 70 or better. This tells you right away, without guessing, that the teacher is failing (both "failing" and flunking) a large number of students: 40 percent of the class. But it also tells me that even 48 percent of the *passing* students are not understanding much of what is being taught.

Now, there may be some underlying variables contributing to these dismal numbers, and these variables should be identified, evaluated, and analyzed. But whatever else is happening, it's clear that there is a problem *inside* this classroom.

The most effective thing a principal can do is to look at these same data-points over three to five years for this teacher. The more apples-to-apples data gathered, the clearer the picture will be.

True, we have already suggested that a principal facing a wide gap in graduation rates should be focused above all in the 1 or 0 of pass or fail, which means to graduate or not to graduate. Why, then, should we break down the teacher's data in a more granular manner?

When it comes to the individual student, the principal should be primarily concerned with passing versus failing, the 1 and the 0. But in evaluating a teacher, an effective leader wants very much to see the data from a more granular perspective.

Look for patterns. In the hypothetical case just presented, we have a teacher flunking 40 percent of his or her students. Assuming that three to five years' worth of data reveals this same pattern, there can be no question that this teacher is failing. Add those passing at 65–69, and the pattern of teacher failure becomes more complete because a majority fraction of those students who pass, do so just barely. Such detailed data tells us that this particular teacher is having a direct negative impact on the school's graduation rate. In other words, granular and extensive as the data may be, the principal's interest in it is *still* strictly in the service of the main mission: to graduate more students, especially male Black students.

Based on the fuller data picture, a committed principal would meet with this teacher and devise a plan to improve his or her performance. The teacher may resist. Some teachers can be defensive or just plain arrogant, especially at the secondary level.

"Look, you've never taught algebra. There are special challenges here."
"That's true," it must be conceded.

I never have taught algebra. I am not an expert in teaching algebra. But I can read three years of data from your classes, and I know that your course-passing results are not aligned with success. I'm not a mechanic, either, but if I'm managing a shop and I see that out of ten cars Joe has worked on, he only repaired two satisfactorily. I can sit him down and tell him, "You're only fixing 20 percent of these cars." Now, as a principal, I also don't have to teach every subject to be able to tell you that you're not meeting the expectations of our school. I have the data, which are based on results.

The data set you ask teachers to track reveals a great deal. But the first thing to look at is the course-passing data. This one result allows you, as a principal responsible for a complex system, to quickly diagnose what's going on in your school and ensure the ship is moving in the right direction. It lets you know where you need to put your support resources. Say you have 150 teachers in your building. There is no practical way you can have frequent one-on-one meetings with 150 teachers. But you can identify the 5 percent who are struggling, and you can reach out to them.

Who are *you* to say that this group of teachers is struggling? How do *you* know?

Because *you* are looking at the course-passing data. With this, you, the principal, know with whom you need to meet. You can have a conversation with each underperforming teacher from the seat of the principal. You cannot meet with 150 teachers, but you don't need to, because not every teacher is having the same problem.

Make good use of your assistant principals. They can deal with routine day-to-day staff issues. But if you see that just 30 percent of Ms. Jones's students are passing, you, the principal, need to meet with her, and you need to find and provide her some support.

By the way—and this is important—if I see that a teacher is killing it, with 90 percent of his students passing, you need to meet with him, too. You need to find out what he's doing, and you need to get him to talk about it and share it, so that you and everyone else in the building can learn from his success.

Patterns

Based on the data, you work with a teacher to improve performance. What, as a principal, you can do with data in the case of an individual teacher, you can also do with the entire school. Principals need first and foremost to know where they are. We must pinpoint our current location before we can lead a journey to someplace better. We can be critical as well as critically helpful only if we have the data. As leaders, we should never justify, make excuses for, or shy away from our data. Acquire it. Understand it. Own it and its consequences.

Patterns, patterns through time, that is what you are looking for. Gather your data, and then look at your data from the perspective of a three-year rolling average. This will allow you to see, with remarkable clarity, how the school has been progressing—where it is on the scale of advancing, stagnation, or decline.

Your top-priority, overriding mission is to increase graduation rates. It is a highly focused mission. But the more data you can collect, the better your odds of accomplishing your mission.

Some folks will tell you that there is some data you just don't need.

Smile, nod, and then look for more data. You will find value in every piece of data you collect. Each datapoint is like a pixel on flatscreen monitor. The more pixels you've got, the clearer the picture. 4K reveals more *life* that 1K.

What You Need to Count

Exactly what data should you be tracking? As for data relating directly to students, track these items:

- Graduation rates for the school
  Current
  Three-year
  Five-year
- Graduation rates for Black males
  Current
  Three-year
  Five-year
- Course passing

Current
Three-year
Five-year
- Course passing for Black males
  Current
  Three-year
  Five-year
- Test score data
  Current
  Three-year
  Five-year
- Test score data for Black males
  Current
  Three-year
  Five-year
- Regents (or other statewide) exam score data required for graduation
  Current
  Three-year
  Five-year
- Regents (or other statewide) exam score data required for graduation for Black males
  Current
  Three-year
  Five-year
- Formative assessment data
  Current
  Three-year
  Five-year
- Formative assessment data for Black males
  Current
  Three-year
  Five-year
- Summative assessment data
  Current
  Three-year
  Five-year

- Summative assessment data for Black males
  Current
  Three-year
  Five-year
- Referral rates for Black males
  Current
  Three-year
  Five-year
- Suspension rates
  Current
  Three-year
  Five-year
- Suspension rates for Black males
  Current
  Three-year
  Five-year
- Expulsion rates
  Current
  Three-year
  Five-year
- Expulsion rates for Black males
  Current
  Three-year
  Five-year
- Student return rates
  Current
  Three-year
  Five-year
- Student return rates for Black males
  Current
  Three-year
  Five-year
- Student attendance data, broken down into month by grade level
  Current
  Three-year
  Five-year

- Student attendance data, for Black males broken down into month by grade level
  Current
  Three-year
  Five-year
- Teacher attendance data
  Current
  Three-year
  Five-year
- Teacher's five-week course data for students
  Current
  Three-year
  Five-year
- Teacher's five-week course data for Black male students
  Current
  Three-year
  Five-year
- Percentage of teachers who make phone calls home
  Current
  Three-year
  Five-year
- Number of home calls teachers make
  Current
  Three-year
  Five-year
- Administration team attendance data (If 30 percent of all of your staff use all of their sick days, this hurts the students and may speak to the culture of the building.)
- Diversity data for students
- Diversity data for staff
- Number of Black males in your school
- Number of students on free and reduced-cost lunch programs
- Relevant social worker and school counseling data
- Frequency of social worker and school counselor meetings with students
- Frequency of social worker and school counselor meetings with Black male students

- Interventions social worker and school counselors make and how frequently
- Interventions social worker and school counselors make and how frequently for Black males

MONITOR YOUR DATA FREQUENTLY

At McKinley, teachers track their students' progress at five- and ten-week intervals. They note by name students who are scoring below the passing grade of 65 percent. We find it useful to divide this group into those who stand at 0–54 percent and those at 55–64 percent. Teachers also note, by number of students, those who are passing. We divide them into 65–74 percent, 75–84 percent, 85–94 percent, and 95–100 percent groups. We calculate the percentage of each teacher's students who fall into each of the performance categories.

By monitoring at five- and ten-week intervals, teachers alert themselves and assistant principals to any warning signs or progress problems. At five weeks, there is time to decide on and implement supportive action. At ten weeks, the report is essentially a summary of the semester's performance, and any interventional support would apply to the following semester.

At five weeks, each teacher performs an analysis of the current data and reports to the assistant principal on what actions will be taken to ensure that goals are met by the next five weeks. The teacher is asked to specify what support is required to ensure that the goals are met. Intervention and support options include:

- Timely reporting to parents of failing students a list of missing work to be returned with a parent signature.
- Referral to student support team (SST) for academic intervention, such as tutoring and extended days, as needed.
- Creation of individual student action plans, with parental input on each plan.

Red, Yellow, Green

We monitor the entire senior cohort at five- and ten-week intervals. The objective of collecting data is not only to understand what is going on with each student but also to enable meaningful, effective action when necessary. The primary objective of the senior cohort monitoring is to promote graduation. We code each student with the colors of a traffic light:

- **Green** signals that the student is ready to graduate.
- **Yellow** signals that the student still needs exams or courses to graduate.
- **Red** signals that the student is not ready to graduate.

Parent letters are sent out and conferences are arranged for students flagged yellow or red.

Yellow students may be entered into a mentoring or other academic intervention program. We also set up "warning checkpoints" to communicate progress with parents or guardians at three, seven, thirteen, seventeen, twenty-three, twenty-seven, thirty-three, and thirty-seven weeks into the school year. We also have a program of motivational speakers.

Red students are assigned individual student mentors and a variety of other academic interventions, with referral to SST as needed for additional support. They are put on the same "warning checkpoints" schedule as yellow students, and they attend presentations by motivational speakers.

In addition to tracking data to trigger and shape actions, we collect and analyze it over three- and five-year periods so that we can get the big picture on where the school is headed.

Chapter 5

Step Two

Goals? Make Them Realistically High

Now that you have collected and pulled together your data, you can use that data to create goals. Goals are intended to motivate performance. That means they have to be worth reaching. And *that* means the goals you set must make a meaningful difference between the present state of your reality and the desired future state. At the same time, these ambitious goals—and they should be lofty, because mediocrity does not create inspiration—must be realistic.

"Realistic" does not mean *modest* or *easy*. Nor does it mean basing goals on the pessimistic and cynical assumptions all too many people bring to the table when it comes to the performance of Black males in high school. But goals should not be spun out of your imagination, fantasies, wishes, or even ideals. The goals you set must be derived from known reality, which means that they should be clearly and honestly derived from historical data. Goals are neither wishes nor guesses. They are data-based markers and metrics of a desired future state.

You urgently need the data from Step One. Why? Because you cannot know where you need to go until you need to know where you are. You cannot get to Point B unless you know where Point A, your current location, truly is. Conversely, once you locate yourself here and now, you can start planning out your destination. At Step Two, the principal, as the leader of the school, has a profoundly consequential opportunity to set the direction of the entire building and the young lives within it.

SPECS

Let's pause a minute here to lay out the overall specifications for a set of goals.

First: The goals you set today should be derived from previous years' data. Using three-year rolling averages provides practical accuracy.

Second: The goals you set must address every academic area within the building, and every student, teacher, staff member, and administrator should know the goals you set.

Third: Your schoolwide goals must be clear, concise, and realistic (i.e., data based).

Fourth: The goals you set must be talked about in every faculty meeting and staff meeting, and in every class. Everyone in every corner and classroom in the school should be participating in one conversation.

SET THE TRAJECTORY TOWARD GRADUATION

The trajectory for Black males in your school will go where you set it. That is what the goals are for.

Let me tell you one personal story.

I played Division IA football at SUNY Buffalo and earned a scholarship as defensive tackle. I was pretty good, but the team I went to was really bad. Our coach was uninspiring. He himself lacked motivation, and that inevitably meant that he was without the ability to get anyone to follow him. It is fair to say, he was a poor excuse for a head coach.

With good reason, I was feeling like a loser. Then, two years into my career as a division IA football player, our team was introduced to a change agent. The university hired a new athletic director. One day after an especially horrible loss—it was in Iowa, and we lost by fifty-two points!—the new AD gathered the team together and announced: "We will no longer lose."

Just like that.

A few weeks later, as the season came to an end, the AD made a bold move. He announced that this would be the final season for the head coach. The firing made national news. Shortly after this, we met our new head coach. We were his first-ever head coaching gig, but he came to us from the National Football League, where he had been a big-time former superstar quarterback.

From the get-go, he brought a new energy to our program. After introducing himself at the very first team meeting of the new year, he announced: "Here is our schedule."

We all just stared at him. He wasn't bringing us news! Every one of us already knew our game schedule, because it was posted—nationally, in fact. This was no big reveal, nothing new.

"Read it," he said.

So, we looked at the copies that had been handed to each of us, looked at the paper from top to bottom. And there, at the end of the schedule, our new head coach had included the championship game. Once he was satisfied that all his players had reached the bottom of the page, he locked eyes on us.

"At the end of the season," he said, suddenly slowing down to form each word clearly and separately, "*this* is where we will be."

The room went silent. And then we all looked at each other. A laugh began to ripple through the team and quickly built to a mocking uproar. It was like *this guy is a joke*. Doesn't he get it? We are the worst team in the country! This was not just a matter of opinion. There were 117 teams in the country, and we were rated 117 out of 117. In fact, we were predicted to lose every game in this coming season, and, as predictions go, it was as close to a sure thing as you could get. But here was our new head coach telling us that in this, his very first season as a head coach *anywhere*, we were going to win the championship.

After we played and lost the season's first game by what must have been thirty points, our coach stood up in front of us.

"Okay, that was a tough game. But here is who we are up against next, and, at the end of the season we will be playing in the championship."

Flabbergasted, we just stared back at him. Doesn't he understand we just lost by thirty? How are *we* ever going to win a championship?

He saw our frustration, of course. For a minute or so, he just looked at us.

"We mourn a loss or celebrate a win for 48 hours. After that, we are done with it. We move on."

Now, we did not go on to experience our Miracle Season. In fact, the new head coach's first season with us was, by the numbers, a complete fail. Well, not quite. We did manage to win one game—just one. Nevertheless, at the end of the season, he told us that, next year, we will be at the championship game, playing for the title.

Come year two, we were not at the championship, but we were a better team, and at the end of year three, we found ourselves in Toronto, playing that championship game. We won.

What happened?

Our leader set a clear goal for us—crystal-clear. Our poor performance during his first season and our obvious failure to achieve our goal did not prompt him to change that goal. It stayed in place. We fell short the next season, too, but did perform better. By season three, we proved that the goal was realistic by finally attaining it.

The moral of the story? The new AD never changed. We did. *He* led us there, but *we* did the changing.

The way this coach sets goals for creating a winning football season tells us a lot about setting goals for improving performance. As the leader of your school, it is imperative that you not only have the data but that you use it to set clear, realistic but ambitious goals. At McKinley, one of the largest urban schools within the second largest urban district in the state of New York, we set our key performance goals 5% higher than the three-year rolling average of the school.

How did this work out?

For the last three years, McKinley had a 75% student attendance rate. We set as our goal an 80% rate. Statistically, we knew that 75% of students, on average, will come to school, so we had done nothing special to contribute to that 75% baseline. But what if we put positive effort behind improving the baseline attendance goal by cranking up our target by 5%?

What we found was that the people in our school worked to align their positive effort toward attaining that goal. They worked toward a number.

Ineffective versus Effective Goals

There are realistic goals and unrealistic goals. There are worthwhile goals and others not even worth the effort. This distinction is less important than it sounds. What cannot be tolerated are *ineffective* goals.

Ineffective goals are ambiguous in that they cannot be counted or touched or tasted or felt. Typically, they have no day of reckoning attached to them, no end date, no deadline, no do-or-die, no make-or-break equivalent of an election day. Consider this goal: "As a school our goal is for Black males to do better in school."

What could be wrong with this? Nothing. Nevertheless, it is an ineffective goal.

"As a school our goal is for Black males to do better in school" is potentially measurable, but it is not competitive. What you need to do is quantify "do better," and then you need to compare that quantity as it exists now to how you want it to exist at some specific future date. You can convert this *ineffective* goal into an *effective* one by

1. Quantifying it
2. And making it competitive, defining (by score) a current level and a target level, to be achieved by a date certain.

It will look like this:

> Last year, our Black males graduated at 29 percent. Our goal for this year is 35 percent by the end of June for their four-year graduation rates.

The ineffective and effective goals do not contradict each other. In fact, they say essentially the same thing. The second version, however, is driven by data, is expressed in numbers—one number covering the present, the other defining a desired future state—which, like the score in a football game, is clear, objective, and compelling.

When the head coach in my story said that we would be in the championship, we all knew that the only way we were getting there was to generate the right numbers, which meant scoring goals. Performance in sports is both competitive and measured by numerical data. Everyone understands the goals. Everyone understands the difference between 7 and 0. Everyone understands the difference between a high score and a low score.

Break It Down

Setting the goal of raising the graduation rate of Black male students requires a simple statement because it is a simply defined, very straightforward goal. Nevertheless, some granular data must go into it.

Let's break it down.

Schoolwork consists of classes that offer different courses, all of which are graded, and only a passing grade contributes toward graduation, whereas failing to pass even a single course prevents graduation. So, create goals, course by course, and track the progress from year to year.

Be Aggressive

Principals need to be aggressive about their goals. They need to lead discussions about them, and to do so relentlessly at every faculty meeting. Practice information overkill. Post your goals in every class. Put them up in the bathroom stalls. Ensure that your goals are front-and-center present and discussed at every faculty meeting.

The principal is responsible for ensuring that no one escapes knowledge of your school's goals. Make them top of mind. As the leader of your building, make it your business to ensure that everyone—faculty, staff, administration, and students—develops a laser-sharp focus on where the school is and where, by the numbers, it is headed.

We know that Black males have the lowest academic performance of any other subpopulation in the country. Inevitably, then, no shortage of people—including teachers, staff, administrators, parents, and even the students themselves—are going to push back on your goals, just as we members of a losing football team pushed back on the goal set by our apparently deluded new head coach.

Don't take that bait.

Just as we know that Black males have the lowest graduation rates, we also know that Black males can and do graduate from high school, enroll in college, and graduate from college. Do not let one set of data distract you from another, equally valid, set.

You must focus, and you must align all the stakeholders in your building with *your* focus. Do this by:

1. Setting clear, ambitions but realistic goals schoolwide
2. Ensuring that every goal addresses every content area as well as attendance
3. Ensuring that goals can be counted, touched, tasted, felt, and seen
4. Trusting staff to reach the goals you set for them
5. Aligning every action taken in the building with your goals

Stick with It

Setting wildly unrealistic goals generally ends in failure. Setting goals without data—guessing and guesstimating—generally ends in failure. And failing to set any goals at all both begins with and ends in failure. But the single most prolific source of failing to reach your goals is quitting before you reach them.

Remember that head coach. He told us we will be in the championship this coming season. Of course, that didn't happen. Instead of changing the goal, he repeated it for next season. Again, we fell short, but we did improve, and the coach set the same championship goal for the third season. That was the season we became champions.

Everybody has experienced the temptation to set goals, only to quit before the goal is reached. Come New Year's Eve, they make a resolution to lose, say, 30 pounds in the coming year. Not a bad goal. It is quantified, and it has a timeline. Aligning with their goal, they go out and shop for workout clothes, start a gym membership, and buy up all the "healthy snacks" they can lay their hands on.

January proves to be a great month for the fitness business. The gyms are always packed. By February, business is down measurably. By April, it is in a deep valley, as people forget their goal and drift back into their accustomed routines.

Not that they are happy about it. They still need to lose that 30 pounds, haven't made a dent in it, and now are not only overweight but feel bad about themselves. Whether you want to lose weight or increase graduation rates for Black males, you need to set a clear, quantified goal and stick with it until it is reached.

Do not deviate one jot from your clear, ambitious, realistic, and measurable goals. In a football game—and in any endeavor—moving the goalpost represents unacceptable change. The only change you will accept is the positive change in behavior and performance. Your success as a principal really should be measured by the rate at which your building achieves the ambitious, data-informed goals you set.

It is hard, but you are not defeated until you give up. So, never give up.

Chapter 6

Step Three

If You Don't Like What's Being Said, Change the Conversation

Transforming failure into success is all about the data. Except when it isn't.

No question: You must track the performance of your students by the numbers, by the piling up of failing and passing grades, and you have to use that data to guide you, your teachers, and the students themselves in improving their performance. There is no substitute for data, but data without love will not get you and your school to the goal you set.

Love, in the context of encouraging academic success, requires showing each student that you care. It requires giving each student time and attention. It requires understanding, honoring, and celebrating every facet of their diversity. Most of all, it requires acceptance.

As data in earlier chapters reveals, acceptance is withheld from Black male students significantly more often than it is from students in other groups. They are bundled off to special education classes at a disproportionately high rate, and they are also expelled significantly more frequently than White students.

Black males are suspended far more than White males. Moreover, they are suspended for minor infractions at higher rates than their White counterparts. Causes for the suspension of Black males often include wearing hoodies, showing "defiance," showing "disrespect," demonstrating "insubordination," or using cell phones. These so-called reasons are not reasons at all. They are abstractions. If your school has a dress code, and wearing hoodies violates the dress code, then a hoodie may be a cause for discipline. But *suspension*? *Really?*

Is suspension an appropriate—a proportionate—punishment for wearing a hoodie? Before you answer this, first make certain that you have a truly excellent answer for this: *What's the matter with hoodies?*

And as for defiance, disrespect, and insubordination, these are sub-jective judgments rather than accusations of concrete violations. What specific *acts* prompted the suspension? Does the act rise to the level of imposing exile? Same goes for "cell phones." Does your school ban them outright? If not, what do your published rules of conduct say about cell phone use in school? What did the student do with his cell phone that warrants suspension?

Repeatedly, for Black males, the message is not the one we educators always say that we want to give: *Welcome to school!* All too often, for Black males, it's *You don't belong in school.*

At the most basic level, then, showing every student love means accepting them all and welcoming them all.

WELCOME TO—WHAT?

When you do welcome all your students to your school, to what, precisely, are you welcoming them? Is it a broken-down place with dismal levels of performance and rates of graduation? Is it a place people—the community, teachers, administrators, parents, and the students themselves—call a "bad" school (and often, the adjective is considerably strong than that)? Is it place where those inside feel like losers? Worse, is it a place where students are made to feel like suspects? Today, metal detectors are in widespread use. There may be no getting away from these. But many urban schools also subject students to elaborate pat-downs and searches by uniformed security officers as they enter the school. It is a corrosive and demoralizing message.

Some messaging is less aggressive, but still demoralizing. Take the label that was stuck on McKinley High when I got there as an assistant principal. It was called a "middle of the road" school or, sometimes, an "average" school. But the middle of *what* road? And "average" in *what* context? McKinley is an urban school, so what we were really being told is that we were "about what you can expect" in a school with a diverse student body.

Well, what does "about what you can expect" mean in such a school? Let's face it. For most people, this meant that McKinley students—students at *my* school—performed at a level expected of a Black school, no better, no worse, but, in the great scheme of things, low-performing. "Middle of the road" was not intended to be an insult, but every teacher, staff member, and student felt insulted or had a good reason to feel insulted or even *should* have felt insulted.

We could have countered this middle-of-the-road assessment with some statistics that showed people that we did not have to stay where we were being put. But the statistics at the time were hardly persuasive, and we need to do something fast to restore or, more to the point, create morale. It could not sound defensive, and it could not come across as an excuse.

So, I recalled that new head coach the SUNY Buffalo football team had hired, and whose story I told you in discussing Step Two. Standing in front of the members of a football team ranked 117 out of 117, he handed us a game schedule ending with the championship. We were flabbergasted. But, three years later, we were champions.

With this in mind, to faculty, staff, students, and parents, I simply proclaimed McKinley High School "The Best School in the Land." What is more, in written communications, in published communications, in everything that came out of our administrative office, those six words were attached to the name of our school: *McKinley High School, The Best School in the Land.*

The new message? "Welcome to The Best School in the Land."

"THE CONVERSATION"

You might protest that slapping a label on a "middle-of-the-road" school did nothing in reality to elevate it. If McKinley had done nothing more than crank out a label, you would be justified in making that call. But what our administrators, teachers, and students did was find ways to live up to the label.

Why begin with the label? Why not start by creating the reality of success and *then* label it?

Two reasons, and they are pretty good ones.

Number one: We did not have any time to waste. Black males, failing to graduate, were leaving school, walking into prison, or finding an early grave. We needed to convey a life-saving sense of urgency.

Number two: We wanted to warmly and enthusiastically welcome all our students. Welcoming them to "the middle of the road" hardly felt like doing them much of a favor. (Hang around in the middle of the road, and you are liable to get flattened by an 18-wheeler.) But inviting them to "the Best School in the Land," well, *that* was really something.

There is a standard conversation that starts whenever people are talking about Black males in an urban school setting. As conversations go, this one is dead tired, drab, and grim, but it is repeated, by rote, ad nauseam.

Goes like this: *Black males have the lowest graduation rates in the country. They get suspended more than any other population in the country. They have the highest incarceration rates in the country.* Subjected to this numbing narrative over and over, we are forced into a negative frame of mind, which prompts us to see Black males as born failures and born criminals. The "middle of the road" becomes the middle of the road to perdition.

Perdition is not where we wanted to send our students. What we wanted was to send them on a path of realistic aspiration.

In Rom 4:17, God is described as one who "calleth those things which be not as though they were." This is a most provocative description. But go back to Genesis, where God sees darkness and commands light. Seeing *not light*, God spoke *light*, the reality he wanted to be.

The great Austrian psychologist and psychotherapist Alfred Adler developed a highly influential technique of inviting his troubled patients to "as if"—to imagine that they *are* the person they wish to be and to act according to that imagined image. It was not intended as a cure, but as means by which a person who desired positive change could begin a journey toward that change.[1]

Alfred Adler understood that we human beings have this godlike power to aspire, to imagine our better selves, to call those things which be not as though they were. Barack Obama was elected to two terms as president by insisting "Yes we can."

So, Step Three in creating higher Black male graduation rates is recognizing that you can no longer tolerate what is being said of these students and, therefore, you act to change the conversation.

Persuade everyone to take their blindsided eyes off the middle of that road to perdition and instead, to look to the sides. There, where few people look, they will find not the all-too-familiar grim statistics on Black males and education, but others, just as true, but often ignored or overlooked.

At the periphery, they will find over one million Black males in college, in this country, right now. They will find more than two million American Black men with college degrees. They will find Black men who are lawyers, doctors, politicians, presidents, CEOs, pilots, entertainers, business owners, authors, educators, and not just inmates or youthful corpses.

When you first look down a road, you reflexively look down the middle. In the case of Black male students, too many of us never look anywhere else. We see only what we are shown, and so we form an instant and indelible negative impression. We acquire an implicit bias based on the media, easy generalizations, blinding stereotypes, and our own laziness—a failure to embrace diversity, honor diversity, and learn from diversity. We do not take the time and make the effort to figure out who each individual is in the time and place in which we encounter him or her. One result is the currently prevailing conversation about young Black males.

Changing the Conversation

If you don't like what's being said, change the conversation. At McKinley, we didn't like people saying ours was a "middle of the road" school, so we changed it to our school is the "Best School in the Land."

Focus only on what you have been told by so many for so long, and you will feel perfectly justified in condemning me for wishful thinking. But look to the left and to the right, and you will find many examples of Black male success. The "middle of the road" is the narrative of those too lazy to look beyond generalization. The "Best School in the Land" is the narrative of those who have heard stories of Black male success and therefore see in the Black male students standing right there in front of them potential heroes of those very stories.

Step Three is to provide your school with a counternarrative to the prevailing unquestioning and unquestioned tale of doom. Give everyone in your building something better than the middle of the road. Give them something way, way better. Head them toward college, which means heading first to graduation. It may not be the obvious middle course for Black male high school students, but, look to the left and look to the right, success is not nearly as rare as you have been misled to believe.

Changing Yourself

Is that all it takes to change the conversation? Just come up with a new label?

No. Replacing a limiting label with a liberating label is necessary, but it is not sufficient. Let's say I had been able to take the "middle of the road" description at its face value, including all the racist freight piled up behind it.

Middle of the road? What did this mean?

We were being told that we didn't have the dumbest kids in America but also that we didn't have the brightest, either. Not great. But is that so bad?

Well, it was a terrible label, a limiting, stereotyping, hateful label—and so was the conversation that went with it. Whatever else "middle of the road" meant, it meant that our kids were not really cut out for college and never would be. This did not align with my values as a man or as an educator.

What to do?

Reject the chatter and instead listen to the voice within you that proclaims your students to be the best and the brightest. Dare to emulate the late Steve Jobs of Apple in its early glory days. Dare to "Think different."

Do so, and you will find no reason why your Black male students should fail to graduate and, if they chose, even go on to graduate from college.

Yes, telling this version of the narrative will put you at odds with the prevailing narrative. Fueled strictly by low expectations, that narrative perpetuates a culture and system of low expectations.

As leader of the school, you, the principal, must decide to create throughout the building an alternative culture, one of high expectations, and to promote the design of new systems to foster and achieve those expectations.

Before you can move—as in *motivate*—your students, faculty, and staff, you must move yourself. How do you really feel about the students in your building? Do you feel that they all deserve a good education? Do you feel that all your students can achieve a high degree of success?

If not, can you be persuaded? Can you find evidence to convince you? If you are already convinced, do you possess the evidence to support your conviction?

In my own case, my own life was all the persuasion and evidence I needed. Too many young Black men from my community dropped out, went to prison, and often died violently. Yet I, who had plenty of difficulty in school myself, not only survived but graduated and went on to college and to graduate school. I am not a freak of nature. If I could find this path, so can others.

So, in my school, I fashioned the new label, starting to tell everyone in my building that we were no longer a middle-of-the-road school but, from now on, were "the best school in the land."

It was provocative. It created a buzz, not only in the school but in the community as a whole. That buzz, in turn, touched off controversy. For decades, people had been calling us a middle-of-the-road school. Here, suddenly, is this new principal telling everyone we are the best.

It is through controversy—questioning the status quo—that you begin to change, that others begin to change, and soon, that everything changes.

You *will* meet resistance, especially from people who take your bold declarations as a dig against them. Be generous with your sympathetic understanding. After all, if you are calling for change, you are saying that something is wrong with the way things are at present.

The controversy at McKinley was by no means all bad. It helped keep the conversation alive. We took control of that conversation so that we could get a particular message across. Most of our students were Black or Brown and mostly in poverty. We wanted them to hear—from us, the adults in the school building—that they did not have to think of themselves as "less than." So, we flooded them with a fresh narrative that labeled them as special, as people with lives that mattered.

For Black and Brown children in poverty, this is a radical narrative. The conversation they have heard all their lives has told them they are "less than," deserve little and can have a damn sight less. Children in urban settings hear about themselves the same relentlessly negative statistics that we hear about them. To them, the task of graduation seems impossible. They not only have to fight their own inadequacy—Part A of the narrative—but also have to butt up against the prevailing theme that they are unworthy, which is Part B.

Again, I have to get a personal in telling the story.

I created a pledge for myself, and every school morning, I got on the PA, and recited it to them, telling our kids that they are the best and that they are the best because they believe they are the best and work hard every day to be their best. Eventually, this pledge caught fire. Every student started hash-tagging that their school was the best and that they were the best at everything they did.

As a school principal, creating and convincingly delivering such a pledge is no easy project, not in an urban setting, anyway. Urban schools are forever drumming into their students the do's and the don'ts, with the accent falling heavily on the don'ts.

- It's don't do this; if you do, you're getting suspended.
- It's don't talk like this; if you do, you're going home.
- It's don't wear this; if you do, you're outta here.

The new narrative I instigated flowed from a philosophy of telling each child that they are special, that you love them, that you care about them, and that you *know* they are *somebody*.

KEEPING IT ALL POSITIVE

Maintaining your positivity is essential to creating and maintaining a positive culture in the school. And this is not easy, because even if you are positive by nature, a positive culture is not the default state in an urban school.

Besides, life does not stop. Principals still have bills, troubles at home, marriages, our own kids, and the reality of being misunderstood by individuals, bosses, and the media. There is unhappy staff and insubordinate staff, and then there is our own personal health. Being positive is often difficult, but it is your mission.

As a leader, it is easy to become and to remain negative. If you chose to become an educator in an urban environment *and* you also want "easy," you chose the wrong line of work. Rethink your career. Rethink your life. It takes grit, intestinal fortitude, and just plain stubbornness to remain positive through negativity. But that is the requirement if you want to change the prevailing conversation for the better and make that change stick.

Begin by taking some time to think about the narrative of your school. What is it now? What would you like to change about it? What would your ideal new narrative look and sound like?

A word of advice. Before you change the prevailing narrative, make the decision to go big. Be better? No. Be the best.

And brag. Constantly. In every article, interview, PA announcement, and grocery store chance encounter with a parent, tell everyone, "Please know that we are the best school in the land!"

Chapter 7

Step Four

Hold Teachers Accountable

Tom Peters is a universally respected management guru, whose two best-selling books—*In Search of Excellence* and *A Passion for Excellence*—have a lot to teach leaders in any field, not just business. These books, Peters himself observes, "are said to have placed renewed emphasis on the qualitative aspects of business—for example, on people, customer satisfaction, nurturing of unruly champions and managing by wandering around." He gladly accepts the appraisal as a compliment but points out that he still harbors "strong vestiges of [his] engineering training" and admits "to being a closet quantifier." He tells us: "I think the soundest management advice I've heard is the old saw: 'What gets measured gets done.'"[1]

Exactly!

Secondary school principals are always preaching the importance of building strong relationships with teachers and students. They preach this, in part, because it's true. But they also preach it because it has been preached to them, and, like a lot of things that are preached, its message seems so self-evidently true that nobody ever pokes around in it, questions it, or even thinks much about it.

Build good relationships with teachers and students. What can there possibly be to argue against here?

Nothing. There's nothing to argue against concerning this piece of gospel, but there is plenty to think harder about. Go deeper. While I wholeheartedly believe in developing relationships among administrators, teachers, students, and, for that matter, parents, community leaders, and other influencers, relationship building between principals and teachers remains special. It is not just about asking them how they are doing and how their families are doing—though it certainly includes such questions. It is also about accountability.

Step Four on the path to improving graduation rates for Black males calls for principals and other administrators to build strong, 100 percent accountable relationships with teachers by making every teacher responsible for hitting all student learning objectives and all the school goals. This means setting goals, requiring each teacher to plan how to reach them, and requiring them to continually measure the progress of each student toward attaining them. Ultimately, each goal set must contribute toward increasing the rate of graduation.

As educators, we principals and teachers must know that we have an impact on student achievement. The only way to *know* this, as opposed to *feel* this, is to set goals and continually measure progress toward them. What gets measured gets done. In my building, every teacher always knew—because I reminded them relentlessly—that they are responsible for attaining all individual student learning objectives and, collectively, achieving the school's performance and graduation rate goals.

ACCOUNTABILITY IS ABOUT VALUE FOR VALUE

In business, the profession of accounting is never a one-way endeavor. A business owner offers a customer a certain product or service of value in return for value received—usually money. Accountability is similarly two-way or, really, a network of such interactive relationships. Teachers are accountable to their students, and their students are accountable to them. Teaching and learning go together as a mutual exchange of value. The teacher agrees to teach. The student agrees to learn. Teachers are also accountable to principals. At the very least, they are responsible for hitting their goals. Principals, in turn, are accountable to teachers to provide the leadership and support to enable or at least facilitate attaining the goals that have been set. One of the great failings of the various government educational initiatives that have been aimed so ineptly at increasing graduation rates has been their demand for what is essentially one-way accountability. These programs hold teachers—even more than principals—accountable for their student's failure to reach goals set by government personnel, yet they provide remarkably little teacher support.

The support principals must give their teachers and staff is both intellectual/professional support and moral support. A high level of morale is not a mere add-on in the struggle to lift graduation rates, it is essential to prevailing in the fight. Every administrator, led by the principal, must thank and celebrate every teacher in their building. They must do this casually, cordially, and often, and they must also do this more formally, with special events of celebration. Have you ever visited a school that does too much celebrating? That's a rhetorical question. Most need to do a lot more.

THE OTHER SIDE OF CELEBRATION

As a principal, you must relate to the teachers in your building in ways that show the high esteem in which you hold them. Esteem is a coin with two sides. At times, your esteem for a teacher must be expressed not in celebration but in creative criticism. Principals must commit to having frank and courageous conversations whenever failures to meet goals are encountered. Never dismiss such failures as mere "slippage." If students aren't passing, the principal should not give the teacher a pass, either.

Like praise, however, criticism must be based on data. Make real everything important by measuring every important thing. The results will not make everyone happy. Maybe it will get you, the principal, in some trouble. But this is what the late great John Lewis called "good trouble," the kind of "trouble" that brings positive, urgently needed change.

Bear in mind that there is very little even the most talented leader can do to "fix" a person, but there is a lot that can be done to change the direction of the data. Improving the rate of passing grades and, thereby, the rate of graduation does not require threats or pep talks aimed at bringing about a transformation in someone's personality. It does call for frank and courageous conversations, but conversations that address data rather than personalities. Fortunately, it is far less painful (for all involved) to tell a teacher that you want to help her/him "to raise the passing rate in their class by x percent before the end of the semester" than it is to say, "you are failing as a teacher."

When you, as principal, meet with a teacher, gather and mobilize the data you have. The trouble with most criticism is that it is a matter of one person's opinion pitted against another's. Data lets us dispense with opinion. As the late, great New York senator Daniel Patrick Moynihan famously said, "Everyone is entitled to his own opinion, but not to his own facts." Data are facts, and facts give both parties in the conversation something objective and neutral to talk about.

As a principal, you need to make the teacher understand that *he* does not have to improve, but the data *must* improve. Is this just another way of saying that he must become a more effective teacher? You bet. But there is nothing personal about it. It's not a matter of being good or bad, talented or talentless, but of looking at the data, acknowledging what needs improvement, and then focusing lessons and teaching tactics accordingly, and ensuring that the lowest-performing students get the help they need.

The teacher need not change as a person—who he is is none of your business—but the teacher does have to find a way to enable his students to perform at levels that will push their grades across the line separating failure from graduation. Focus the conversation on finding those ways with the goal of getting the data everyone—principal, teacher, student, parents, community—wants.

PRINCIPALS, TEACHERS, AND STAFF ARE ACCOUNTABLE FOR MAKING EVERY STUDENT WELCOME IN THE SCHOOL

Nothing is more important than data. Just remember that while data is necessary to creating academic success, it is not sufficient for that task. We also must love our students, which means we need to care for them and care about them.

The single most caring and loving thing principals, teachers, and staff can do is to ensure that they are continually creating an environment for students that is welcoming and challenging. This is important for everyone in the classroom, but it is especially critical for Black males, for whom the default setting in all too many classrooms is anything but welcoming. As we have seen, suspension, special education classes, and even expulsion are wielded against these students far more and for far more trivial infractions than they are employed in the case of any other group.

While everyone is accountable for creating a welcoming environment throughout the school, it is the principals, the leaders, who must step up and set the tone. As leaders, we principals must find or invent as many ways as possible to broadcast in everything we say and do a message of welcome—of welcome to all teachers, students, administrators, janitors, parents, community members, and other stakeholders. School must be focused on inclusion, integration into the neighborhood, the nation, society, and civilization itself.

Your school is a portal into everything good and wonderful that our ancestors, brothers, and sisters have created throughout all time. It is also a portal to the future, through which your students may pass to platforms and professions from which they can contribute to the great store of skills and insights and ideas that continue to advance civilization. As a nation, we cannot afford to bar this portal against anyone. So, we must all contribute to an endless rolling message of welcome.

Ensure that teachers, students, and everyone else feel welcome within the building. How? The whole strategy can be expressed in a single sentence consisting of an imperative verb and a plural noun: *Build relationships*.

Start this way. Say good morning or good afternoon to everyone you encounter in the building. Accompany your greeting with a smile.

If this sounds ridiculously simple, well, the fact is that it's harder than you might think. It requires mindfully focusing on others, which we perpetually busy educators often find difficult to do. It takes remembering to say good morning or good afternoon. It takes energy. You may just want to get from the office to the restroom, but it's up to you to marshal the energy and the bladder control to greet everyone you meet en route.

If you call this a "greeting," you must understand that a greeting is a *welcome*. If your mind runs a bit more formally, you may think of the "good morning" and the "good afternoon" as *salutations*. That word comes from the Latin *salutare*, which means paying your respects to someone. An effective greeting conveys both welcome *and* respect—joy in seeing *that* student in your building as well as your promise to respect *that* student for everything he or she is, looks like, and says.

If you doubt the power of the greeting/salutation, think about the last place you visited where you felt unwelcome or ignored. Chances are, it started when no one greeted you.

Along with dismal graduation rates, low-performing schools have one thing in common: an unfriendly culture. Adults don't speak to adults, adults don't speak to students, administrators are always so busy they don't feel they have the time to say "good morning" or "good afternoon," let alone start a quick, friendly conversation with anyone. The result is a school environment that is chronically tense, untrusting, and, in fact untrustworthy.

If a place is cold, indifferent, or downright unwelcoming, it becomes a place from which you run away not a place you run toward. If students are not present in school, they cannot learn. If the teacher is physically present but mentally and emotionally absent, the effect is much the same: students cannot learn. A caring, loving, welcoming environment creates a warm culture that keeps teachers and students engaged in the learning process.

Build on the greeting.

In addition to saying "good morning" and "good afternoon" to just about everybody whose eye you happen to catch as you move through the building, make sure you speak with every teacher daily. Throughout the day, visit every floor and make an effort to say hello to every teacher, every teacher's aide, each administrator, and whomever else you encounter.

Famed leadership expert Tom Peters has a name for this. He calls it "management by wandering around."

And it works. If it sounds easy, be aware that it does take time and effort, but it certainly is not a difficult strategy—at least when things are going reasonably well.

When things are not going great, when the pressure is turned up high, you, as principal, feel like doing what most people feel like doing when the chips are down. You want to dive under your desk, curl up, and wait for the situation to magically transform itself.

But you don't. Instead, you suck it up, show yourself, and greet everyone.

Whatever you do, in smooth sailing or storm-tossed waters, please try to remember that the salutation runs two ways. When you bid someone good morning, pause for a response and take time to acknowledge it. From this point on, get inventive. Think about ways to build opportunities for teachers, staff, and administration to get together. The most natural way to get together is to eat together. Picnics, lunches, and even retreats help build a culture of welcome and value.

BEYOND THE GREETING

One of the principal's most valuable assets is his or her voice. Principals are in a position of power. Their very title identifies them as Number One: the Principal Person. Use that power.

Nike has a voice. It sounds like this: *Just do it.*

McDonald's has a voice: *I'm lovin' it.*

If sneakers and ground beef can exercise the power of their voice, shouldn't a principal be able to do the same?

Good corporate slogans tell consumers what the organization and its products stand for. Principals need to figure out what the organization they lead stands for. Then they need to express it. A "middle of the road school"? No. Not *our* brand! Not *our* voice! "We are the best school in the land."

If challenged—*Really!? Well, how does* that *work?*—come back with a *because*: "We are the best because we believe we are the best, and we work hard every day to be our best." That is a recipe for creating a culture of success. Just add data and stir in some love.

TO BE ACCOUNTABLE IS TO BE ENGAGED

Research shows that when Black male students feel engaged and when their teachers care enough to hold them accountable, they create academic success.

Teachers are accountable for creating within their classroom a culture that fosters rather than discourages engagement. Principals are accountable for creating within their building a culture that fosters engagement and a willingness to be accountable. Principals must hold their teachers accountable for being fully engaged in *teaching*. And teachers must hold their students accountable for being fully engaged in *learning*. As effective principals make the teachers in their building feel valued as well as accountable, so effective teachers make their students feel valued and accountable. This enables success.

But what is "success"?

We might validly answer that success means many different things to many different people. Your concern as principal, however, is raising the graduation rate in your school, especially among the most imperiled group, Black male students. This makes success easy to define. In your school, "success" is reaching the goals the school accepts in common. Topmost among these is graduation.

Maintaining Teacher Accountability

The principal's job is to support teachers, retain their enthusiastic engagement, and hold them accountable. These are three distinct functions, but they are intimately interconnected. Holding teachers accountable is key to supporting them and ensuring their engagement.

Goals are indispensable to creating teacher accountability. Start with a goal. What is the goal of your school?

Initially, the answer is simple and should be universal. The goal of every school is for every student to graduate.

But within the big wheel of this goal are numerous cogs. The goal of graduation entails creating course-passing goals for each class. If students do not pass their classes, they do not move on to the next course. If they do not move on to the next course, their morale and motivation diminish. Without appropriate intervention, many of them, left to their own devices, will disengage from their studies and the whole academic setting. If this happens, say, in the ninth grade, these students' eventually dropping out will likely happen without that ninth grade teacher ever being aware of it. In many of our high schools, twelfth grade suddenly reveals a whole cadre of students unaccounted for. With that—*boom*—the big goal of every student graduating high school on time explodes and evaporates into so much thin air.

Slack jawed, we ask, *How did so many students just slip through the cracks?*

The answer is that nobody tracked the data. *What gets measured gets done.* The grim corollary to this axiom now becomes obvious: *What does not get measured gets lost.*

So, the course-passing goal for your students must be set high, and the progress of each student must be measured and tracked, producing data that will be invaluable to create improvement. The necessity of tracking should spur engagement.

At McKinley, every teacher was issued a five-week course-passing data goal sheet. Since grades were assigned every ten weeks, at the five-week mark, our teachers would break down, class by class, how their kids were performing academically. They provided data on how many students are in the home room, how many students are passing, and how many students are passing at what levels.

This tracked data becomes the stuff of conversation if, say, you have twenty-five students in a class, of whom only ten are passing and, out of that ten, just three are passing with a grade higher than 70 percent. The conversation, between teacher and principal or assistant principal, is how to improve performance.

Another accountability goal used at our school is the New York State Regents exams. These are set of several exams that students must pass to graduate from high school. If you are a student and you do not pass the Regents, you will not receive a high school diploma.

We set a goal at our school for the teachers in each department to hit a certain level of passing Regents exams for that department. To create a realistically ambitious goal of improvement in the rate of passing exams, we looked at the three-year rolling average of the last three Regents exams and, each year, added a five percentage-point bump, to give the teachers a realistic aspirational goal.

By way of incentive, all teachers were told that the principal's evaluation of their work would include how their students perform on the Regents.

Evaluation of performance is important in just about every job, of course, but principals and teachers alike share two much more consequential dimensions of accountability when it comes to how well or how poorly their students perform on the exams needed for graduation.

One dimension is on a personal level. Suppose your students are failing to pass the exams required for graduation. As a teacher, you need to ask yourself: If my students are not learning while I am teaching, then am I *really* teaching? It is a disturbing question, and, for that very reason, it motivates a good deal of healthy soul-searching, which may result in teachers making essential professional decisions. Most of the time, they find ways to become more effective teachers.

But there is the even more profound and urgent dimension of our accountability. Principals in urban high schools often find themselves attending the funerals of their Black male students lost to gun violence. Like my childhood friends who died violently, they had in common the lack of a high school diploma. Better to have a hard conversation with a teacher than to be obliged to console a crying mother who has just buried her child because we—principals and teachers—had low expectations for her son.

Chapter 8

Step Five

Resources—Prioritize, Focus, Allocate

The principal is the orchestrator of a school's success. Think about that word. The principal does not compose the music but does assign the instruments and their roles, making sure that all the priorities are accommodated and all the players—administrators, teachers, students, and staff—understand and carry out their roles.

Step Five is all about orchestration: prioritizing, focusing, and allocating the school's resources toward achieving all the goals that have been set. Assigning the topmost priority is, as they say, a no brainer. It is the goal of graduation. First and foremost, you need to allocate resources to facilitate achieving your target for that goal.

DON'T CURL UP WITH THE STATUS QUO

Even well-run schools are hectic places—dynamic—with a lot of activities. In the midst of the continual swirl, principals and others in the building are sorely tempted to seek a little peace and quiet, a little stillness. But one of the most valuable pieces of advice a superintendent ever offered was to resist this temptation.

"Avoid maintaining the school's status quo by doing the same thing over and over with the resources you have," he said. "Always get better."

Principals need to look closely and comprehensively at how their school's resources are allocated and how they might adjust that allocation to better serve the goals they set for the school.

Take a fresh look at your available resources and how they are being allocated. The keyword here is not *resources* but *allocated*. Resources can be tremendously valuable, but their value is diminished or lost entirely if they are not wisely *allocated*—not merely made available or applied but made available and applied where they are needed most. Resources for any school are scarce—there is never as much as you want—so you have to leverage every resource tactically and strategically to maximize and even multiply its effect.

At McKinley, we had partnerships with various colleges, which provided our students with free tutors from their teacher-education programs. Now, such partnerships a terrific for three reasons. First, there is the tutoring. Our partner colleges would send some of their students to our school to tutor our students. Second, the mere presence of *college* students in our building helps to make college look like a real and realistic possibility for our students. They experience working with college students, and they come to understand that they can join their ranks. And third: it did not cost us a dime.

What could be wrong with such a resource?

Nothing.

And we had several college partnerships within our building. Without question, free tutoring is a great resource to have—when properly allocated.

But it became apparent on close inspection that numerous tutors were coming by to help our students in several serious content areas but none of our students showed up to receive the tutoring. The college kids arrived, full of enthusiasm, eager to help out. We had students who could really benefit from their guidance and assistance—desperately needed it, in fact. And yet the providers of the service and the consumers of the service rarely got together. This wasteful situation, it turns out, had gone on for years.

Nothing was done about it. It was our status quo.

As principal, I reached out to all teachers, especially those who were missing their passing goals by wide margins. I had the college tutors *pushed* into those underperforming classrooms to assist with instruction in the very classrooms where they were most needed. If the students would not self-select and come to the tutors, we would bring the tutors to the students—and not randomly but based on need as demonstrated in the course-passing, test-passing data.

This example illustrates a simple lesson in allocation of resources:

- First, identify your resources.
- Second, determine where they are most needed.
- Third, get them there.

BY NATURAL LAW, TIME IS A FIXED RESOURCE. SO, ALLOCATE IT STRATEGICALLY.

In some schools—ours included—built into teacher schedules is something called "common planning time" or the equivalent. It is intended to provide an opportunity for every content-area teacher to work collaboratively with other teachers in *common planning* to create strategy and tactics aimed at improving student performance, which, of course, means raising the rate of graduation.

At McKinley, it turned out, "common planning time" was too often used as a time for teachers to hang out and chill. This was a basic misallocation of the resource of time, so we changed the rules and expectations, so that common planning time was no longer free time but a resource expressly allocated to working on lesson plans based on formative assessments, which were intended to ensure that we were taking the necessary steps to get more of our students to pass more of their exams.

Once the teachers were aware that the principal was paying attention, they began using the time to collaboratively apply the assessments to their lesson plans, so that students would be focusing on building the specific strengths they needed to pass their courses.

Principals need to take a fresh look at one of their greatest resources, assistant principals. At McKinley, these were some of the busiest people in the school. But that left them little time in their schedules to provide the guidance and help teachers needed.

The problem here was not an allocation of time, it was an insufficiency of assistant principal bandwidth. There just was not enough of *their* time available.

The answer was to buy more time.

We hired an instructional coach, whose job was to provide every teacher with the high-quality assistance they needed. While it is true that no amount of money will buy more than the twenty-four hours that are in a day, you can recruit specialists who have some of their time available. One way to tell when you need outside help is to take notice when key people *inside* your building have all of their time booked. Outsiders may be brought in to provide certain expertise unavailable inside, but they, sometimes, what you really need is *their* time.

Money Talks

Money is not a dumb resource. It talks to you, and you have to be willing to listen.

As the leader of the building, a principal must review the school's entire budget and find ways to allocate funds to purchase items necessary to achieve your priorities. One of the major priorities established at McKinley was to move our math scores upward.

At the time, we were classified as a "struggling" school, which is a classification just one small step above being classed as a "poor-performing" school. Math is an especially weak area for us, and that meant it was one of our best levers for elevating our performance. Improving math scores would give us the biggest bang for our buck. Math, therefore, was announced as a priority.

But you cannot just announce such a thing and then do nothing about it. When you set a priority and establish a goal, you must act on it—and quickly, before it fades from the top of everyone's mind. That is when our math department revealed a piece of stunning news. The teachers reported that if money could be found for them to purchase new calculators, we *would* see an increase in students' test scores.

You cannot throw money at every problem and expect a solution. In this case, however, money *was* the answer, and now was the time to let the money do some talking. A close review of our school budget revealed that we had $15,000 allocated for "books and supplies." Incredibly, this line item had not been used for years. In other words, each year, we effectively gave the district back $15,000.

Insane. But no more.

We spent all $15,000 on new calculators for our math department, and the department came through with a 10 percent to 15 percent increase in test scores—each year—for all of our students.

Principals must dedicate themselves to finding resources and being smarter with them, using them directly to raise course-passing rates, ensure graduation, open up futures, and save lives.

Take a Close, Hard Look at Your Resources and How They Are Allocated

When an administrator tells you to review your budget, don't jump to the conclusion that she or he is asking you to cut back, to slash the budget to make do with less. Instead, look critically at your budget. Separate it from the status quo. Meticulously inventory your resources, including funding, free resources, and time. Then get inventive with what you have.

Partnerships with colleges are good to have, especially if they are free. College students are given an opportunity to gain valuable experience, students are given an opportunity to get much-needed help, and they also are put into a position where they can relate to a real-live *college* student. But be sure you recognize that even *free* tutoring programs are not worth the time they take if the tutors and the students most in need don't get together. Be inventive. Take a hand in things. Intervene and push the tutors into wherever they are needed. Encourage them to lean in proactively.

By the way, college partnerships are not the only resource you have for tutors. Your students are not just consumers of education, they can be producers of education as well. Develop peer-to-peer tutoring programs. Both tutors and tutees (yes, that *is* a word) will benefit.

Allocate Your Teachers Both Tactically and Strategically

What's inside a school building? The most obvious content items are students and teachers. By all means, select your best and most willing students as peer-to-peer tutors, but never forget that your teachers are also a resource in need of strategic allocation.

Principals and other educational leaders must be highly intentional—keenly strategic—when it comes to issues of professional staffing and allocation. Use your data to identify your highest-performing teachers. These are not necessarily your most charismatic teachers, your nicest teachers, your best-liked teachers, or even the teachers who strike you as most talented. They are, first and foremost, those who consistently achieve or exceed their performance goals.

You have the data.

Use it to identify the highest-performing teachers and then deploy—allocate—them to where they are needed the most, which is not with your "best" students, but with the underperformers, those at most risk of not graduating.

Another aspect of managing your school's teacher resources is to monitor and act upon all vacancies. Vacancies in teaching and other staff must be filled promptly. Make it your business to ensure that the teachers you do have do more than simply teach their classes. They must also use their time to commit one-on-one conversations with their students, especially the hard conversations about getting into position to graduate. They must also commit to planning collaboratively with their students as well as other teachers.

Chapter 9

Step Six

Discover Their Big Why

Teaching and administering teachers is not a business. It is both a profession and a calling. Nevertheless, we can learn from business.

Successful businesses carefully cultivate their human capital. They evaluate employee performance with both direct observation and objective data. Take sales and customer service employees. The manager observes how they relate to customers. This empirical but subjective data enables managers to make reasonable subjective judgments about employees' manner, demeanor, how they treat customers, and so on.

As important as these assessments are, what is more important is performance metrics as measured by sales. How much revenue does a given salesperson generate for the company?

Collecting, tracking, and analyzing sales data is not just a way to keep score, but to evaluate performance, including which selling tactics and behaviors work effectively and which do not.

Another thing business teaches us is that the most successful salespeople not only produce the best numbers, but they also advance themselves within the company. They are committed to their success and the success of the company. Put another way, they are intensely goal oriented.

Top-performing employees have measurable goals. *I will sell* x *widgets this month*. Such metric-based goals are important, but the main thing is that top performers achieve these goals by knowing what they themselves are about. For them, the job was not a matter of punching in and punching out. They are not waiting for something better to come along. They have a vision for themselves, regardless of whatever position they hold at the moment, and this enables them to develop skills, knowledge, experience, and a mindset that are entirely portable.

In business, "portable skills" are personal assets. They belong to the employee, not to the company. They walk in with the employee in the morning and leave with that person in the evening. Such assets can be taken anywhere and used to build a rewarding career or, more to the point, the succession of rewarding careers that typically make up a financially successful and vocationally rewarding life.

In 2009, the noted motivational speaker Simon Sinek published a book called *start with why*. It is a great title—partly because it is so obvious.

Just think about it for half a minute. *Why* is one of the most basic words in the language, yet most people use it less often than the two other words that often go along with it, *what* and *how*. In fact, most people use *what* far more than either *why* or *how*.

Take students, for instance. If you are a teacher, you are in the business of *why*. You want your students to ask *why*, and a big part of your job is to help them to answer that question and then encourage that answer to lead them to asking more *whys*.

The thing is, *why* is the seed. It's the question and the impulse that starts every journey of genuine learning. Both the teacher and student are in the business of learning, and their stock in trade is *why*.

So, start with why.

Sinek's book has an almost laughably simple diagram consisting of three concentric circles. The "golden circle," he calls it. The innermost circle is labeled *why*, the middle circle is *how*, and the outer circle is *what*. He uses the diagram to illustrate the perspective of how successful leaders influence their organizations to what he calls "transformations."

Now, that's obviously a bigger word that *why*, but the two are directly connected. In business, you want to *transform* your start-up company into an innovative, profitable dominant brand. Sinek says that, before you can plan *how* to make this transformation and *what* you must have to make this transformation, you need to start with *why*. *Why am I in business? Why should I be in business? Why do I want to lead the dominant brand in my industry? Why do I want to work so hard to make this transformation?* Answer these *whys*, and you will locate the energy and direction toward the transformation you desire and need.

On a more personal level, *Know your Big Why.*

How big is Big? Here are examples of questions to ask in order to know your Big Why: *Why am I in this job? Why am I in this profession? Why was I put on this earth?*

We want students to arrive at their Big Why by asking and answering this: *Why am I in school?*

The following applies to each of us—principal, teacher, or student—but I will address it to "you."

In thinking about your life, your career, our purpose, your role, your place in the world, your place in the community, you need to start asking a bunch of *whys* and then decide which among them is your Big Why: your controlling purpose, your motivating goal, your highest priority. Whatever else your Big Why is, it is the thing—the prize, the force, the goal, the passion—you believe is worthy of driving you.

Only after you have answered *why* in terms of articulating your Big Why, can you productively move on to *how*, by asking *How will I answer my Big Why? How will I achieve my top goal or goals?* The answer to these questions, in turn, leads enables you to ask *what*. What *do I need to do the* How *so that I will realize my Big Why?*

It is a process by which you—a sales clerk behind a counter, an entrepreneur, a principal, a teacher, a student—can give greater focus, urgency, method, and intentionality to all that you do.

Back in 1927, when the British physicist Sir Arthur Stanley Eddington wanted to explain why time moves in only one direction, he came up with a metaphor he called "the arrow of time." Let's borrow this to emphasize that the sequence from *why* to *how* to *what* is like arrow of time. It is a progress that moves in one direction only and must start with *why*—not just any *why*, but your Big Why.

THE PROBLEM WITH STARTING AT THE END

"Start with why" is an imperative sentence. Imperative sentences provide directions, instructions, or advice. They are also sometimes commands, orders, directives, or requests. Most are simple sentences: "Turn right," "Take the garbage out," "Start with why." As such, they are easy to comprehend.

Yet, as I said, comparatively few people actually do start with *why*. More people start with *how*. Even more start with *what*.

Or at least they try to, only to discover a big, big problem with starting at the end: You go no further. Why? Because it's the end!

Let's say you assign your students to "write an essay on Maya Angelou's *I Know Why the Caged Bird Sings*."

You may get no questions about the assignment, but, more likely, you will get some, and they will be something like:

"*What* do you want us to say about it?"
"*What* part of the book should I write about?"
"*What* websites can I use?"
"*What* are you looking for?"

Or:

"*How* are you grading this?"
"*How* can I write this?"
"*How* long does it have to be?"

The one question you will probably never be asked is "*Why* should I write this essay?" And, if you do get such a question, you might answer, "Because Maya Angelou is a great writer" or "Because it's a requirement of the course" or "Because I told you to do it" or "Because you might learn something."

These are not incorrect answers; however, they have nothing to do with teaching or learning. But, then, starting with *what* or *how* has nothing to do with teaching or learning, either. Teaching and learning start with *why*.

Starting with Why

Starting with why does not require that a teacher literally starts every lesson with "Why are we . . ." This approach would be inefficient because it is not nearly big enough. In terms of presenting the overall material in a particular course, a teacher should focus on the *why* followed by the *how* and then the *what*. In each class, this sequence is a great way to begin the semester. But you should also go bigger.

The *why* we need to focus on *throughout* high school is the Big Why that each student must discover for herself or himself. *Why am I in school? Why should I study? Why should I work for four years to graduate?* Those are all good starting questions, but they are still, by themselves and individually, not big enough.

Your top-priority job as a principal, as the leader of the school, is to create a physical, mental, emotional, and cultural space in which each of your students can discover their "Big Why." From this discovery comes the inner motivation to answer—affirmatively, positively—all the other *whys*. Discovering your Big Why is important to all students, but to no group is it more urgently *imperative* than to Black males.

From birth through high school, few Black males ever look for, let alone ask, find, and answer, their Big Why.

It is not their fault. They have simply never been invited to do any such thing. The notion has never been put into their heads. Too many grow up in a world without *whys*. Their environment is filled with *hows*—as in, How am I going to get by? and How am I not going to get my ass kicked today? And there are *whats*: What will happen to me next? What do I need to do to belong to some group that will help me to get by?

The point is that poverty, danger, racial and cultural stereotyping, and outright racism fill the world of many young Black males with so many *hows* and *whats* that there is no room left for any *whys* at all.

Choices?

For many young Black males, these are limited or pretty much nonexistent, at least if we are talking about choices likely to lead to positive outcomes. Graduating from high school immediately broadens the range of available choices. Failing to graduate clamps down and forecloses upon them.

CREATE SPACE FOR BLACK MALES
TO DISCOVER THEIR BIG WHY

Do young Black males disproportionately have their aspirations and goals frustrated and denied?

No. I would say it is much worse than that, because so many of the Black males who drift in and out of our schools do not even have aspirations and goals to be frustrated and denied. A profusion of short-term *hows* and *whats* has blocked out the horizon on which the *whys* are found.

Young Black males are not frustrated in their dreams because, in too many cases, they have learned not to dream.

School leaders, especially those in urban schools, have the responsibility to transform their buildings into spaces for Black males to discover their Big Why. How can anyone succeed in any career, profession, or enterprise if they don't even know *why* they are trying?

One of the most demanding endeavors any of us embarks upon is education. Elementary education can be challenging, but, as we all know, high school is far more demanding. It calls on an intellectual, emotional, and social independence and self-efficacy that many Black males have had no opportunity to develop. Teachers, parents, and principals become frustrated and even angry because so many of these students demonstrate indifference to succeeding in high school.

We need to ask a variation on "How can anyone succeed in any career, profession, or enterprise if they don't even know *why* they are trying?" It is this: *How can you succeed in any endeavor if you don't even know why you are being asked to succeed?*

"Creating space" for students to find their Big Why does not require an imitation of Genesis, the creation of something out of nothing. Even the worst-performing schools have a lot more than *nothing* to offer. Just as a principal must inventory the resources of the school, as I advised in Step Five, searching for money, time, personnel, outside partnerships hitherto ignored, unused, underused, or simply misused, and then find ways to productively leverage these assets, so school leaders need to examine and assess what their educational space has to offer.

Having fully answered the question, *What are my school's current resources?* The next step is to devise ways in which the available resources can be used to transform your school into a space in which your students can discover their Big Why.

At McKinley High, this transformation began by telling everyone—students, teachers, parents, the public, and administrators—that We Are the Best School in the Land.

After all, in such a superlative place, who could fail to find a space in which to discover their Big Why?

But we went further.

Everyone in the school was invited to get more specific, more granular. Besides being the Best School in the Land, we asked, What is McKinley High School?

The short answer was that it is the largest career technical education school in Buffalo, which, by the way, is the second largest city in the State of New York, second only to New York City. This is a big deal, and we wanted everyone to appreciate it.

But what, precisely, does it mean to be such a formidable technical education school? Put it this way: Our students can literally build a house from the ground up. They can learn plumbing, electrical, HVAC, print media, horticulture, and aquatic ecology. They can even attend an Urban Teacher Academy Program. And this is in addition to all the standard academic classes, including many specifically intended for college preparation.

What this depth of resources offers is opportunity, multiple opportunities for our students to discover that they can excel as something other than being a football player or a basketball player, which—yes—even in this day and age is where many young Black male aspirations both begin and end.

We can go even further toward finding our Big Why.

Discovering that your choices are far more numerous than a couple of career categories that offer vanishingly few paths to actual careers is transformational. It opens the way to students thinking about the future in real-life terms by connecting their present environment—their school—with possible versions of their future environment: the "real world." To the degree that principals can reveal to teachers, parents, and, above all, to students that there is a real connection between the school's curriculum and viable paths to success in the real world, those principals have begun to orchestrate not only success in their building but far beyond in both space and time, into the wider world and the future.

This is how we school leaders can throw open the door to the Big Why of each of our students. Make a persuasive case for your school's connection to the real world, the world your students inhabit, the world in which the future is uncertain, dim, or even menacing. Devise ways in which to demonstrate to them *why* they are doing, in school, what you are asking them to do.

But don't just throw open the door to that Big Why. Make your curriculum intensely relatable to the real world, so that you start tearing down the walls that separate the business of the school from the business of the world beyond it. Demonstrate the urgent connection between the school-present and the real world-future.

McKinley is fortunate to have a tremendous career technical education program. If your school does not have such a trades orientation, find other ways to expose and celebrate your connection to the real world. Work with your teachers, students, and the community to create project-based learning opportunities, such as:

- **Start a business**—with the objective of profitability, documenting all aspects of the venture.
- **Redesign your city for the future**—addressing anticipated problems as well as opportunities.
- **Redesign democracy**—identifying the current strengths and shortcomings of this form of government, building further on the first and correcting the second.
- **Plan, create, and tend a community garden**—that addresses food needs.
- **Address the problem of "fake news"**—with a project to develop evaluative standards to identify bias and separate fact from fiction.
- **Plan the ideal social media platform for teens**—considering current platforms and improving upon them.
- **Write and produce a short documentary video**—on a school or local subject.
- **Create internship programs with local businesses.**

As schools must welcome students of diverse backgrounds through their doors, so these schools must embrace every productive aspect of the world beyond their walls. While we welcome, honor, and care for Black male students in our schools, so we want to ensure that our schools welcome the entire outside community and that our schools are, in turn, welcomed by that same community. Students need to see their school experience as an experience of the real world of adult responsibility and opportunity.

Chapter 10

Step Seven

Work, Workout, Rest, Smile, Laugh, Hug Your Family, Keep Your Mind and Body Healthy

On September 6, 1901, the namesake of my school, William McKinley, was fatally wounded by an anarchist named Leon Czolgosz while visiting the Pan-American Exposition just a short distance from where the school now stands. The twenty-fifth president died eight days after he was shot, which meant that his vice-president, Theodore Roosevelt, was now the twenty-sixth president of the United States.

Teddy Roosevelt was a legendarily dynamic man—naturalist, adventurer, author, rancher, Rough Rider—and a dynamo of a president. An icon of vigorous health and inexhaustible energy, he famously advocated what he called living "the strenuous life." Yet he had hardly started his life that way. In fact, to read the story of his childhood is to read a painful tale of a brilliant, curious, and enthusiastic youngster plagued by persistent illness, including terrible asthma and chronic digestive problems. When the boy was twelve, his father sat him down for a frank talk.

"Theodore," he began, "you have the mind but you have not the body, and without the help of the body the mind cannot go as far as it should. You must *make* your body. It is hard drudgery to make one's body, but I know you will do it."

Theodore's mother, an eyewitness to this speech, recalled that her son reacted with a half-grin, half-snarl. Then, "jerking his head back, he replied through clenched teeth, 'I'll make my body.'"[1]

Teddy Roosevelt's father gave him not just wise counsel but loving counsel and life-saving counsel. The boy began vigorous workouts at a local gymnasium. He also hiked and swam and hunted and climbed hills and even mountains. He made his body, and he made his life.

So far, we have dealt mainly with improving students' intellectual achievement to earn passing grades in demanding high school courses so that they can graduate into lives with a genuine future. In setting down the seventh step toward increasing the rate of Black male graduation in our schools, let's not forget what Theodore Sr. told Theodore Jr.: "Without the help of the body the mind cannot go as far as it should."

You probably know this from personal experience. You just don't feel right unless you get a certain amount of physical exercise or do something, unrelated to your job, that you enjoy and that refreshes and recharges you.

For some, it is a vigorous daily workout at the gym and a good rest at night. For others, it is a walk with dog or playing catch with your children. Whatever it is, we all need to understand that mental health is linked to physical well-being.

This is a fact of life, and, so, Step Seven, is to do whatever it takes to get healthy in mind and body and stay that way.

Go to the gym, get adequate rest, eat well, and find time to fully disengage from the hard work of school. This advice applies to teachers, administrators, and students. But let's focus especially on the teachers and administrators. If you are in a diverse school, a school rich with minority students, you know that the work of teaching, like the work of learning, is especially arduous. Take into consideration that, in an urban school, the work of education is also the work of saving young lives, and you have a calling that is infinitely rewarding but also both physically and emotionally demanding.

So, use your vacation time and other time off. Really *use* it. Spend time with your family and, if you possibly can, take time off when *you* feel you need it most.

People these days talk a lot about the "work-life balance."

If you are tired of hearing that phrase, it is because it sounds so stingy and miserly. The time you spend with your family or other loved ones and friends should not be so meticulously balanced against the time you spend at work. You don't have the time and energy and commitment to squander on such mean mental bookkeeping.

Few ambitions are less rewarding than becoming an accountant of the emotions. Instead, when you are at home, devote 100 percent to the people you love, and when you are at school, give your students 100 percent.

Don't waste your mind and break your heart trying to balance the ledger book of your energy and devotion. In whichever arena you find yourself—at school or at home—just go flat out 100 percent.

But understand this. The job of education need not be joyless drudgery. On the contrary, acquiring knowledge and skills is one of life's few truly *absolute* good things. School, therefore, should be joyous. In the morning, when you walk into the building, start looking—immediately—for the multiple opportunities this environment offers to smile and laugh.

Is the work of teaching and learning hard?

You bet it is. Working to improve your students' performance and your own performance is some of the hardest work you can possibly take on. But that just means you need to smile broader and laugh louder.

Science has amply demonstrated that no medicine is stronger than laughter. For one thing, it draws people together in the ways that make healthy physical and emotional changes in our bodies. Physicians have all the data that proves it. Laughter boosts your mood, strengthens your immune system, measurably diminishes pain, and helps to protect you from the physically damaging effects of stress. Moreover, no medicine or other therapy works nearly as quickly or more reliably than a good laugh when it comes to centering yourself, lightening your mental and emotional load, inspiring hope, and connecting you to others. Laughter creates a mental, emotional, and physical environment that keeps you focused, alert, and engaged. And it is a great antidote to irritation and even outright rage.

Laughter is one of your school's greatest resources, and, best of all, it will never show up on any budgetary line. If you want to be a better teacher, principal, or student, exploit every available opportunity to laugh. Hear yourself and others laughing, and you cannot help but realize that the hard work we put in during the school day is nevertheless a joyous and loving labor.

Chapter 11

Step Eight

Red, Yellow, Green—Target Student Intervention

Data is *not* about anonymity or uniformity. The eighth step toward increasing the rate of Black male graduation is targeted student intervention, which means identifying those students who are at risk for not graduating with their cohort and intervening in a timely and a precisely targeted manner to ensure that the student has what he needs to graduate.

While our top priority is to raise graduation rates, which means getting the at-risk students across the line and across the stage, we do not neglect our high-performing students. In fact, we challenge them all the more, putting the emphasis on AP classes with an eye toward college. From the beginning, we set expectations high—and we do this where others have reflexively—out of social habit—set them low, acting on the self-fulfilling prophecy of underperformance and failure for Black male students.

NINTH GRADE AND TWELFTH GRADE ARE KEY

The difference between elementary and middle school on the one hand and high school on the other is more profound than many adults realize. This is the case for all students, but none more than Black males. They come into high school at thirteen without any concept of what high school demands from them. Days in elementary school and middle school were very structured, and the learning process was pretty much one-sided. Teachers taught. Students learned or failed to learn. Either way, they were constantly told what to do. By contrast, high school is not compatible with such passivity. The learning experience is not rigorously structured by the teachers.

In high school, students are suddenly asked to work more independently. They are expected to do this with less teacher supervision, more academic freedom, and more autonomy, transitioning to classes without oversight. Although data demonstrate that Black males, on average, struggle in secondary schools, teachers and principals persist in their belief that, at age thirteen, all students should be able to work with very little guidance and supervision. The high school's leadership is essentially saying to incoming students, you are now free to be successful.

The problem is that middle school is far more a continuation of elementary school than it is a preparation for high school. This means that the entire transition from a hyperstructured passive learning environment to a looser environment in which students must take far more responsibility for their academic success must be accomplished entirely in ninth grade.

The traditional approach to the ninth grade experience is to go easy on students, to keep expectations low. The problem with this is that if you approach students with low expectations, they will thoroughly satisfy *those* expectations by performing at a uniformly low level.

Front-load the ninth grade. Think of it as creating a "freshman academy," an experience that provides this cohort an opportunity to bond and to stick together and perform together. Put your highest-performing teachers at this grade level. Ask them to provide this cohort with heightened expectations coupled with more supervision to produce greater independence.

Through eighth grade, students have been comfortably riding tricycles. Now, all of a sudden, they are being put on bicycles.

They must master those brand-new bikes, but they do need training wheels. And that is what the ninth grade provides, in the form of close teacher supervision and monitoring. As training wheels help a kid learn to move from three wheels to two, so ninth grade must introduce students to the "high school way."

In the ninth grade, teachers must apply the first seven of the ten steps. As they do this, they must carefully monitor, individually, the entire cohort.

Create a spreadsheet that tracks every student in that group. This is how many kids we have in the Class of Four-Years-from-Now. Layout the goals for the cohort. The top priority is to graduate, of course, but, at McKinley, we added to this an ambitious provision: everyone in the cohort will graduate with what is called in the New York State system an Advanced Regents Diploma, one of the highest degrees a student can earn in an American high school.

That's right. We demanded that Black males, representatives of a group that, statistically, struggles in high school, aim for the highest diploma possible. If we aim for the stars and hit the moon instead, we will still be in a better place than if we never got off the ground at all.

Set the bar high and do everything in your power to support attaining that bar. This *action* creates a winning, high-expectation culture.

The goal is not to get Black males to graduate from high school. But do not hesitate to append another goal to this, the goal of ensuring that this set of students will also be competitive in college.

Before I came to McKinley High, the school's goal was for the cohort to achieve the bare minimum required for graduation. Full disclosure: This should be the priority goal of every urban high school for the simple reason that is the goal that saves lives.

But *also* aim higher, knowing that if you *set* the expectation to a bare-minimum level, the *best-case* scenario is achieving the bare minimum. That is just not enough margin.

In fact, some—maybe many—of your students will not make the bare minimum. They will fail, they will become disengaged, they will drop out, and they stand a fair chance of dying violently and young, either with or without having first gone to prison.

By setting a lofty goal, you create a mindset—within the entire cohort—that motivates students to compile, by their junior year, a record of performance that prepares them for college. Such a record is not created passively. Students need to *want* this. So, in their students' freshman year, teachers must front-load them for success, orienting and equipping them for a performance in high school that will open the doors to college.

In ninth grade, students should be provided a lot of support to set them up for success. In most high schools, students take the PSAT in their sophomore year to prepare them for the SAT in their junior year. At McKinley, we began the practice of having students take the PSAT in their *freshman* year, mainly to get them accustomed to this gatekeeper examination for college.

It is of great value to encourage students to visualize that college goal from their very first year in high school. It needs to look and to feel real.

At McKinley, having given the PSAT during freshman year, we have sophomores take the SAT. It won't be the last time they take it, of course. In their sophomore year, it is practice for taking it in their junior year.

By doing the PSAT in ninth grade and the SAT in tenth grade, the cohort will be better prepared for taking the SAT in their junior year, when it will be used as part of their bid to gain admission to a good college. Think of the ninth and tenth grades as "packaging" your students for high performance in the eleventh grade, including on the SAT, so that they will enter twelfth grade with college a thoroughly realistic goal.

In one sense, the freshman academy idea is to create a productive, high-performing transition into both the sophomore and junior years. The idea of transition assumes that there will be much room for improvement, that ninth grade is a kind of ramp-up to the rest of high school. There is truth to this vision, but, at the same time, we want our freshman students to achieve and maintain as high a GPA as possible.

Why this emphasis?

As significant as the psychological difference between elementary/middle school and high school is, perhaps even more consequential is the difference in calculating GPA. We don't often think about this, but it is critical. From K through 8, grade averages reset every year. But from grade 9 through 12, GPA is cumulative. Freshman year may be a transition, but it counts just as much as the other three years.

Students often have a hard time fully appreciating the significance of a cumulative GPA. It is the responsibility of the adults in the building, the administrators, school counselors, and the teachers, to get performance as high as possible as soon as possible. So, give your students demanding classes early on, and give them maximum support, including providing them with your highest-performing teachers.

Remind them continually that your expectations for them are of the highest: You are going to college or trade school or the military. You are not going to the fast-food restaurant, the unemployment line, prison, or the grave. You are preparing to have choices—good choices—in life.

From ninth grade, give them the rigorous classes upfront to make sure they are getting everything you need. Do not settle for doing just enough to get by.

Let your freshmen know that the administrators and teachers in their school set the tone. Show and tell them: We will tell you what our expectations are.

When you come into our school, we are telling you that you will take your SAT in your sophomore year. We are telling you that you are going to take it again in your junior year. We are setting a tone to prepare each of you to have way more than the bare minimum of credits required for graduation.

At McKinley, this is not a *conversation* we have in the ninth grade. It is a *declaration* and a *demand*, but it is also a promise on our part that we are going to support each student with our best teachers and every other resource we have or can think of.

And we know the support is needed, because Black males are coming into the school with an educational deficit. They are coming in from behind, and they are coming in on a wave of negative expectations based on research.

What is required is a demand for the incoming students to meet high expectations accompanied by a promise of a high level of support. In all too many schools, the only demand is that students meet the minimums. Instead of an offer of wraparound support, the message is *this is the ninth grade. Time to be an adult.* The thing is, those incoming ninth graders need intensive support to begin their transition to adulthood. At McKinley, we began giving it to them.

The main goals for McKinley freshmen are to get their highest GPA possible in earning the necessary credits to be considered a sophomore.

Senior year is the final reckoning. The first job of administrators and teachers is to ensure that nobody falls through the cracks, succumbing to senioritis, the infamous lethargy that often sets in when there is a feeling that you are in the homestretch. Teachers and administrators need to ensure that seniors remain engaged.

Fortunately, senior year offers a variety of events and privileges that are typically concentrated near the beginning of the year. Principals should revise the senior-year calendar as necessary to distribute these privileged events *throughout* the year rather than packing them upfront. Senior breakfast, dances, senior trip—all of these should be treated as incentives, positive reinforcements, golden carrots, each keyed to meeting academic performance milestones.

Does this sound childish? Well, most of us adults encounter an incentive every two weeks in the form of a paycheck. Incentives are the way of the real world.

RED, YELLOW, GREEN FOR SENIORS

We noted earlier in this book that, at McKinley, we have a system to monitor the entire senior cohort at five- and ten-week intervals. The objective is not merely to understand what is happening with each student but to do so in time to take meaningful action with academic interventions targeted precisely on what students at risk of not graduating needed.

The entire senior cohort is represented on a spreadsheet, with each student coded with the colors of a traffic light:

- **Green** signals that the student is ready to graduate.
- **Yellow** signals that the student still needs exams or courses to graduate.
- **Red** signals that the student is not ready to graduate.

A red student is one who has not met the school and state requirements to become a senior. Even though he is in the fourth year, he has fallen behind his cohort and, until the needed credits are earned, he will not be eligible to graduate with his cohort. The yellow student is officially a senior but is still in danger of failing to graduate. Intervention is still called for. The green student is on track to graduate, but now is the time to push and encourage that student to excel.

Parent letters are sent out and conferences are arranged for students who are flagged yellow or red. Additionally, yellow students are entered into a mentoring, tutoring, or other academic intervention program. Red students are assigned individual tutors (drawn from partnerships with teacher training programs in our partner colleges) and a variety of other academic interventions, including referral to SSTs as needed for additional support. The team may include teachers, the principal, school psychologist—whatever personnel is needed, on a case-by-case basis.

The objective is to do whatever is needed to move a red student to yellow, and a yellow student to green. We focus the necessary resources for intervention on these students. One thing to also note is that, as a principal, you must have an accurate number for your cohort. If you do not have an accurate account of your cohort numbers, it makes it impossible to add in the interventions your students need. Your exact numbers should be able to be gathered from the state department of education.

Targeted Academic Interventions

Let's say the spreadsheet identifies a senior who has not passed the state exam in algebra. We have at this point a *senior* who is taking a *freshman* course, and that is not the answer to getting him over the line and into the graduation ceremony. Now, senior year offers a lot of potentially slack time, but study hall is not going to get him the help he needs in algebra and neither are the other carve-outs of time we find in senior year, such as OJT (on the job training programs that allow a student to leave school early or come in late).

No, no. This is an emergency. For lack of a passing grade in algebra, a life is in danger.

This student did not do what he has to do, which is pass the class or pass the test or both. So, as principal, I am going to see to it that he gets academic intervention precision-targeted to address his deficiency in algebra.

We offer a specific math academic intervention, a special course that helps students with concepts as well as study skills—everything they need to succeed in the course. There will also be one-on-one tutoring, extra reading, extra support. This student will have to work hard, but we will give him the targeted support he needs.

We tell the student this: "You *are* going to walk across that stage—with your class."

We also make a promise to all parents: "Your child *will* walk across that stage, even if I have to drag him across."

We embraced a no-fail mentality, an always-win mentality, a we will work until the job is done mentality, and an every student succeeds mentality.

As mentioned, we partner with nearby colleges that offer teacher-education programs. They furnish student tutors and tutor-mentors, who come to our school and work with our students who are in need. The tutor-mentors get valuable teaching experience, it costs us nothing, but it may well be the extra step that gets our student across that line and across that stage come June.

For the kids who are stuck on algebra, for instance, we may marshal the talent, knowledge, and skills of three or four future math teachers, so that we have four or five adults in one class, supporting as many as thirty kids.

Most schools—McKinley included—don't exactly have a ton of resources, so principals need to think outside the box and also get all hands on deck.

The failure of Black males to graduate from high school is a national crisis. This was a pandemic before anyone ever heard of Covid-19, as Tyrone C. Howard put it in his 2014 *Black Male(d): Peril and Promise in the Education of African American Males*: "A close examination of the current state of education for African American males in Pre K-12 schools reveals that these students' underachievement and disenfranchisement in schools and society seem to be reaching pandemic and life threatening proportions."[1] The situation is dire and urgent.

In addition to targeted tutors and classes during the school day, you may need to do what we did: send targeted students to night school, offered in your building.

For a student who lacks a certain number of credits required to graduate, night classes can be invaluable in helping to "recover" credits he should have earned earlier—in the case of algebra, in his freshman year.

In some cases, an approved computer program—self-administered, no teacher required—can be used to let the student to recover needed course credits on his own.

The point is to monitor the cohort in terms of red, yellow, and green, identify the students who are not ready to graduate (red) and who are ready at present but in danger of slipping through the cracks because they have not met this or that requirement (yellow). Having identified the deficiencies, we get those students everything they need to recover the missing credits or pass the needed classes and tests.

Tell them that they *will* walk across that stage, come June.

Of course, we know that, regardless of what we say, most of the burden is on the student. He's the one who needs the credits, and neither the principal nor anyone else can give them to him.

But what a principal can do is to ensure that the school offers him all the support he needs. If he fails, if he drops out, it is a tragedy, but a principal needs to know that he or she did everything possible to prevent it, as did everyone else in the school.

Increased Rigor for High-Performing Students

The single most important thing McKinley, as an urban school, does for our community and our nation is to graduate students, especially our Black male students, at rates substantially higher than throughout the rest of the country. That saves lives and enables futures. It also builds the brand of our school as a place of academic excellence. It transforms our building into a source of pride, inspiration, and hope for everyone in it, students and teachers, as well as for the surrounding community.

But we also want academic excellence at the top end. We have many students who perform exceptionally well. If you are a first responder, an EMT, and you are called to the scene of a mass-casualty disaster, the first thing you do is triage the injured, identifying the badly hurt, those in imminent danger, and you treat them first, leaving the others to look after themselves, at least for a time.

To an extent, teaching in an urban school requires triage. We identify those students at greatest risk and we flood them with targeted support. But you must be careful not to take the triage metaphor too far. Teaching is not a mass-casualty disaster, although it may at times feel like one. You cannot afford to ignore your top performers just because they are in little or no danger of failing to graduate. You want to offer them greater challenges—and not just offer these, but push them, making sure that these students go into higher-level math and science courses, AP courses, honors courses.

Many Black male students don't consider such avenues of achievement for the simple reason that they are all too willing to meet the low expectations set by others. Black males often don't get the opportunity to excel because we don't believe they can excel. For us at McKinley, the answer was to create an educational environment in our school, The Best School in the Land, that offers only the very highest expectations for all of our students.

TESTING STRATEGIES

As educators, we want our students to learn. Quite rightly, the idea of "teaching to the exam" seems cynical to many teachers. And, in fact, it is a transactional strategy, intended to produce short-term results rather than contribute, long-term, to a student's education. Yet the fact is that to pass a course you must pass exams, and to graduate, you must pass state exams. In our educational system, which is plugged into our society's system of employment, there are many gates, and exams are the gatekeepers.

No, we don't teach to the exam, but we do devote time and effort to testing strategies. Since so much rides on tests, we want to make sure that we give our students ample support on how to achieve high performance on tests by coming to the test with as much of an advantage as possible.

A lot of students choke on tests. Recognize this and do something about it. Devote major effort to build confidence in test-taking. Give your students the strategic and tactical tools they need to maximize their results.

This starts with empowering them to make choices. For instance, when a student sits down to take a test, he typically assumes that it is a task that must be completed question by question. In fact, most evaluative tests do not require working through them in serial fashion. Our approach is to empower students to survey the test and make the best use of the limited time allotted by first identifying the questions they are confident in answering. We advise them to play to their strengths by answering all these first. Get them in the bank before going back to the questions that occasion more doubt and require more struggle.

You must not cheat on an exam, but you must not surrender to it, either. A test is a tool in the educational toolbox. We advise our students that they need to practice and, as with any tool, learn how to use it and how to use it skillfully.

We sit down with students who have trouble with tests, and we review the student's test with him. We identify what he does well and what needs improvement, and then we target those areas. What specific tactics and strategies will help *this* student with *this* test? We also stress the importance of self-talk, that internal monologue all of us conduct continuously. It is tied tightly to our sense of self, so it pays big dividends if we can help students turn their self-talk in a positive, affirmative, confident direction. Most often, we need that direction to turn *against* all that they have been told all of their lives and turn *toward* the idea that they are the best, brilliant, and of academic excellence. That is why it is imperative that we say our pledge, tell the students that they are the best and that our school is the best.

THE SCHOOL COUNSELOR'S ROLE

Let's pause here to acknowledge the crucial role school counselors play in monitoring students as they progress toward graduation. Our counselors coordinate all the performance and student progress tracking. They see to it that the cohort spreadsheets are complete and accurate. They send out the trouble alerts, and they do so in a timely manner, that is, when there is still time to intervene.

It is also the counselor's job to conduct "graduation conversations," to sit down with each student and calculate the balance sheet toward graduation, identifying what milestones have been passed and what milestones still loom ahead. Where deficiencies are present, the counselor coordinates with the student, teachers, and administration (usually at the level of assistant principal) to support him, giving him all that we have to offer to ensure that he graduates with his cohort.

WE CARE

At every grade level, good teachers, effective teachers, care. In elementary and middle school, that caring is largely manifested by administering a disciplined program to the students. At these grade levels, there is a lot of forming up classes in lines and marching them from place to place. This kind of guided discipline characterizes the pre-high school experience. But in high school, the caring is far less about administering programs than it is about helping students become productive in their new circumstance of autonomy and personal responsibility.

In elementary and middle school, teachers are often in their students' faces. In high school, the teacher's energy and effort are more directed toward creating independence and *self*-efficacy. This can make it seem as if high school teachers just do not care, that their message to students is *you're on your own*. But nothing could be further from the truth. Every adult in the building must care, but must also inform that caring, that loving spirit, with data. Thus guided, the caring is targeted, and it is aimed at greatly outlasting the four years of high school. It is about giving each student something they can take with them as they move on to college, a vocation, a profession, a life beyond our school building.

Chapter 12

Step Nine
Reimagine Discipline

The ninth step toward graduating more Black male students is to reimagine discipline in high school.

To "reimagine" is not to "soften" or "loosen" or "forget about." Discipline in any organized endeavor is about achieving and maintaining effective focus and purpose, and it is also about safety and security.

Discipline in school should be about transforming the external, punitive, sources of discipline into internal discipline that each student carries within himself or herself. This transformation is like any other teaching-learning relationship. The adults in the building, teachers and administrators, endeavor to impart knowledge, method, and values to the kids in the building. Discipline is a body of knowledge, a method, and a set of values. Discipline is therefore teachable, and like everything else teachable, it is far better taught persuasively rather than coercively.

In short, discipline is about training a behavior. In an interview with a reporter for the *Buffalo News*, I explained that, as a principal, my job was to train students in the discipline of success. "Rather than beating kids down," the reporter wrote, "he wants to lift them up because that's what people did for him. 'Our discipline is the discipline of success, said the McKinley High School principal."[1]

Principals and teachers need to think of discipline not in terms of punishment and reward but as training a behavior. This was the approach learned in my own training as a therapist. Most educators have no such training; therefore, the idea of discipline as training a behavior simply does not occur to them.

The truth is, most of the time, educators are being trained more than the students. Teachers and administrators call out misbehavior and issue a penalty on the spot. They do this because they have observed that, in the presence of authority, students will behave. The adults in the school have essentially trained themselves to be guards or monitors. This, in turn, has trained the students to understand that they can behave any way they want, as long as no one is looking. This is not training a behavior that the student internalizes.

As an educator, you must get yourself inside the heads of your students. They have to internalize your message, carrying it with them so that it sticks. They need to understand how discipline benefits *them*.

Remember, I created a school pledge, which I would announce over the PA every day: "We are McKinley High School, the Best School in the Land. We are the best because we have the best students, the best teachers, and the best admin team." Then I would continue: "I am the best because I believe I am the best, and I work every day to compete to be *my* best." I ended by borrowing the name of our sports teams: "I am a McKinley Mack!"

My students repeated the pledge frequently. I would stop random kids in the hall and ask, "What's our pledge?" If they could not recite it back at me, we would recite it together.

More important, if I observed a student misbehaving, I approached and asked, "What's our pledge?" Then I would point out to the student that the behaviors he was acting out now do not align with our pledge. And I was always specific about naming the *behaviors*, the actions, not speculating about attitudes or feelings.

This is better than saying something like "Stop doing that." True discipline, internalized discipline, is not a list of don'ts. It is a list of do's. Point out to any student whose particular behaviors do not align with the school's rules or values—or its pledge—how to adopt behaviors that *do* align with it. Point students in the right direction. Do it positively, with love as well as diligence and always, always, always with high expectations.

What is the highest expectation? To believe that each student you lovingly discipline will behave in the right way, the way aligned with success, *eventually*.

Beyond pedagogical issues regarding the teaching of discipline, there is the immediate function of discipline, which is to ensure that the school is a safe and secure environment. Your students need to feel cared about and cared for.

They need to feel welcome in the building. To the degree that they do not feel safe and secure, they are justified in feeling unwelcome and even abandoned.

SUSPENSION IS NOT THE ANSWER

Training, relentless and relentlessly loving training, is the key to discipline. Yet the action to which many educators, especially in urban schools, resort both first and last is suspension. No doubt, suspension is a decisive action, and there is a measure of satisfaction in taking decisive action. The problem, however, is that suspension is an incredibly ineffective way to train behavior. The most effective way to train behavior is to have and to keep that student in school, so that you can teach him how to behave *in school* to get the benefits of what being in school has to offer.

We discussed suspension earlier and more than once in this book. Try this. Try to make your very first thought concerning suspension: *Suspension is not the answer*. This is important because—in the case of Black male students— teachers, administrators, parents, and many students themselves believe that suspension *is* the answer. In fact, this mindset does not even frame suspension as the last resort. Rather, it *is* the answer, which means that it is thought of as pretty much the *first* resort.

By the numbers, as we have seen, Black male students are suspended at far higher rates than White male students or, for that matter, students of any other gender, race, or ethnicity. Moreover, they are often suspended for infractions that, in the case of White students, result either in reprimand, detention, or other relatively minor consequence. Often, for White students, minor infractions are met with no consequence at all. The only conclusion to draw from this, therefore, is that, in the case of Black male students, suspension is indeed the go-to option.

Never mind that this application of this penalty is inherently unjust and disproportionate. The more egregious problem with suspension is that the best you can say about it is that it is ineffective. Far more usually, it is harmful and even diametrically the opposite of what is called for or needed. Remember: virtually the default situation is that Black males come to school feeling that they are unwelcome and that they do not belong there. In part, this is a product of an impoverished, typically violent, and often generally disadvantaged urban environment.

There is systemic economic inequality in our nation, and it is coupled with systemic racism. This is a terrible thing, and it is a state of affairs that must be fought against and changed, but there is a wrong and an injustice that is even worse. It is manifested when the leadership and teachers in a *school* fail to ensure not only that *every* student feels welcome but that feel they are exactly where they belong.

We educators cannot shoulder all the blame for society's shortcomings and sins. But the world *we* create within *our* building? Well, that's on us 100 percent.

Mistreated, some kids shrivel up, shrink down, and do their best to become invisible so that they might avoid suffering more pain. But, mistreated, some youngsters become enraged, act on their anger, and more generally act up and act out. Throwing these young people out of the building does nothing but confirm them in the reason for their rage. They are not welcome. They are not wanted. In fact, they are not fit to pass through the school doorway, which is a portal to success in the real world.

Suspension is the realization of what so many young Black males feel, namely, scorn and rejection. Make no mistake: there *are* instances of school violence that call for the violent person to be removed from the building. In such instances, suspension may be the first step in a sequence that might involve counseling or other intervention, even up to and including the justice system. But such instances of a clear and present danger to the safety of the school community are rare. Far more often, the behavior bears no resemblance to criminality, and the appropriate disciplinary action, therefore, is not to disengage a student from academics by exiling him.

In the vast majority of cases, the first resort—that is, the action most likely to produce a positive, beneficial outcome—is to leave suspension, that tired old traditional big stick of academic discipline, on the shelf. Suspension is the nuclear option in our educational system—in other words, stupidly, senselessly destructive.

The last thing an underperforming student needs is to be disengaged from academics. All students need to be in their classes, and no category of students needs this more urgently than Black males. Now, having chosen to keep your hands off the big stick, turn instead to restorative discipline.

Restorative Discipline

We are accustomed to living with a criminal justice system that uses essentially one consequence to punish crime: incarceration. The U.S. Bureau of Justice Statistics reports that, in 2018, Black males accounted for 34 percent of the total male prison population, white males 29 percent, and Hispanic males 24 percent. At 2,272 per 100,000 Black male residents, the imprisonment rate for Black males was 5.8 times as high as for white males (392 per 100,000 white male residents).[2]

If you hear in the disproportionate rate of Black made incarceration a booming echo of the disproportionate rate of Black male school suspension, you are *not* jumping to conclusions. The rate at which Black males are incarcerated reflects our nation's systemic racism. And that is terrible. But perhaps even worse is that incarcerating *anyone* is rarely an effective solution to crime. It certainly does not benefit the prisoner, but neither does it benefit society. To be sure, there are some people who commit acts so dangerous that separating them from the rest of the commonwealth is a reasonable and prudent thing to do. But, in most cases, a better consequence of criminal action is to impose a restorative sentence.

The truly injurious effect of a crime is not that a law was broken. The law feels no pain. The truly injurious effect is that one person hurt another. Restorative justice views many criminal offenses as instances of interpersonal conflict between the offender and the victim. Instead of inflicting retribution on the offender, therefore, why not better serve both the offender *and* the victim by shifting the consequence away from retributive punishment and toward making things right—toward restoring stability, restoring equitable balance, and righting the wrong?

Restorative justice looks for ways to allow the offender to repair the effects of the conflict. Sometimes, nothing more than a formal apology from the offender is required. More often, that apology is accompanied by payment of reparations to the victim. It takes some creative thinking to come up with a fair restorative solution, but, when well crafted, such a solution has a better chance of restoring justice than does the blunt force of punishment. A restorative consequence restores—as much as possible—what a victim has lost as a result of a crime. At the same time, it restores the offender in that the consequence does call for discarding him or her. Instead, the offender is given the opportunity to restore his own conscience, his own membership in the community, by at least attempting to make things right.

More and more progressive schools have adopted and adapted restorative justice principles. Indeed, it is usually simpler to formulate restorative solutions in a school environment than it is to do so out on the mean streets of the "real" world. Generally, transgressions between students or between students and teachers truly are interpersonal conflicts and can be resolved by agreements brokered between the parties involved. The idea is to affirm positive, constructive, and productive interpersonal relationships within the building without excluding, exiling, or shunning anyone. The objective is to preserve the personal dignity of everyone in the building for the simple and compelling reason that everyone belongs there and is valued there and is cared for there. Moreover, at school, everyone has the right to be treated fairly.

Restorative discipline creates consequences intended to foster mutual respect and understanding. The perspective of everyone involved in a conflict is heard and considered in a "restorative conference" aimed at resolving the conflict by restoring positive interpersonal relationships within a safe environment. The product of the restorative conversation should be a clear and agreed-upon plan for restitution, for what needs to happen to set things right and restore positive relationships.

Schools that support restorative disciplinary practices have certain characteristics in common.

- Within the building of such schools, a good feeling prevails, a positive, inclusive climate.
- These schools broadcast a continuous message of welcome and belonging.
- They are places where students, teachers, staff, administrators, and visitors all feel safe.
- In these schools, students feel a sense of belonging and do not fear that they are at risk of being excluded.
- Students experience productive and satisfying learning relationships with adults in the school and with one another.
- Teachers and administrators collaborate on creating culturally responsive pedagogies.
- Teachers, administrators, and students practice cultural proficiency and celebrate diversity within the building.

- Teachers and administrators reject "deficit explanations" for students' failures. They do not doom the student to failure because of what the student may lack in background or preparation. Instead, they make plans to address such deficits.
- In these schools, daily attendance is high, both among students and teachers. People want to be there.
- Students' educational, social, and emotional needs are recognized and met.
- Behavior expectations—the school's rules—are agreed on, clearly specified, and shared with everyone in the building.
- There is respect for individual differences.
- Policies concerning bullying (including cyberbullying) are made explicit and fair.
- The physical environment of the school is clean and well maintained. This is an important aspect of demonstrating caring about and caring for everyone in the building.

We may ask whether the conditions, qualities, and values just enumerated are *prerequisites* to making restorative discipline effective or are the *results* of having a policy of restorative discipline. The answer is that the relation between the values of the school and the policies of restorative discipline are symbiotic. They work together in a virtuous circle.

Students Need to be in Their Classes

The benefits of graduating and, what is more, graduating with one's cohort, are so great and the consequences of failure so dire that students, teachers, and administrators cannot afford to waste a single minute of the school day. Students need to be learning. They need to be in their classes.

Is that Really a Violation?

Taking time out of the day to impose a punishment should be regarded as a serious decision with serious consequences. The very first thing a teacher and an administrator must ask is *Has the student actually violated a rule?* Recall from our earlier discussion that Black males are not only referred to the main office more often than any other group, but they are more often referred for highly subjective "offenses," such as speaking loudly, being disrespectful, or being defiant.

Are these truly violations? Does, for example, your school have a rule that says, "Students are not allowed to be disrespectful?" Or "Students are not allowed to be defiant?" Of course not. Rules concerning behavior need to address specific actions, such as refusing to do an assignment, using racial epithets, threatening violence, and so on. What one person considers "defiant" another may recognize as asking a legitimate question or making a legitimate complaint.

Genuine breaches of the peace and violations of clearly stated rules should never be ignored, but behavior that cannot be described objectively in terms of an action or a specific behavior cannot be deemed to violate anything.

Instead of sending a student to the office because you feel "disrespected," why not tell the student how he has made you feel?

"I feel that you are disrespecting me. Is that what you meant to do?" And then ask why the student did that. Instead of looking for a reason to punish the student or to reject or exclude him, why not make an effort to address the problem—or at least air the grievance?

ISS

Sometimes a student's bad behavior is disrupting the class and thus taking valuable time away from the other students. If such a situation does not lend itself to a rapid resolution when it occurs, ISS may be considered. This keeps the misbehaving student in school, doing work, but temporarily isolates him from the rest of the community in the building. It is a kind of timeout, a pause that may succeed in interrupting and cooling off impulsive or bad behavior.

ISS should never be used as a stand-alone solution to a discipline problem. It should be used as a way to get to the root of the misbehavior and to encourage positive and productive behavior, and it may also be used to discourage repeat offenders. To accomplish these goals, ISS must be accompanied by academic support, mainly in the form of the availability of a teacher in the detention room. ISS should provide time for the student to work on assignments, and it should be structured to keep students engaged.

LOVE AND DISCIPLINE GO TOGETHER

Discipline is a gift. It is guidance in focus, self-control, and harnessing creativity. Teaching discipline is a loving act, an act of caring. In the short term, intelligent, strategic discipline is a ticket to academic success, which means that it is one of the keys to graduation. Since graduation is often the difference between prison and premature death, on the one hand, and a free and rewarding life on the other, discipline, imparted in the selfless spirit of love, saves young lives.

Chapter 13

Step Ten

Celebrate . . . Everything!

The research shows us that principals have a powerful but indirect impact on student achievement. Always bear in mind that principals ultimately work through teachers. The principal orchestrates success, and a big part of that orchestration is to create a culture of celebration, which trickles down to the students. A culture of celebration is a culture of the positive. In our emphasis on data, it is all too easy to fall into the habit of looking for the negative, that is, for what cries out for improvement. This is important, but it is equally important to look for the good.

To create a culture of celebration, principals should instruct and encourage the teachers in their building to spend more time rewarding the behaviors and performance they want to elicit than they do criticizing and complaining about what is not working or not working well.

Never ignore anything that needs improvement. In fact, *everything* needs improvement. *Passing* performance should be improved to *high-passing* performance and high-passing performance to *excellence*. But nitpicking only gets in the way of what we principals must do, namely initiate and lead a true paradigm shift.

Ask a high school principal, *Do you know who your top thirty students are in each grade level?* Don't expect an affirmative answer. But ask if they could name their top ten "challenging" students at each grade level, and you will likely get an ample answer.

If you are a principal, ask these questions of yourself. While you are at it, try these two questions: Who are your fifteen best teachers versus your top fifteen worst teachers?

If the negative is easier for you to answer than the positive, don't beat yourself up. This pattern is normal or, at least, usual. The wanting naturally sticks in our craw more readily than the satisfactory or better. That is why it takes a paradigm shift—an act of imaginative will—to find compelling reasons to celebrate. So, don't beat yourself up. Instead, if reasons for celebration don't effortlessly leap to your mind, take more time and spend more imagination looking to celebrate the successes of your school.

Set this aspirational goal: everything we do in school should be regarded as an affirmation—an affirmation of what, exactly? I invite you to make your own list, but I can offer some of the items on mine. An affirmation of—

- You
- Me
- Each of us
- Our beautiful diversity
- Our common humanity
- Our learning community
- Our neighborhood
- Our city
- Our country
- Our future
- The liberating and empowering power of education
- The liberating and empowering power of data: truth
- The liberating and empowering power of love
- Freedom
- Life
- And all that we do for ourselves and one another in this school building.

There is injustice, uncertainty, and outright danger in the lives of our students, especially those in our urban schools. There is also the cacophony of a lot of negative voices, and not all of them are wrong. A "normal" school day can be hectic, to say the least. Sometimes, that day becomes nearly overwhelming. No wonder that it is so easy to lose sight of all that we have to affirm.

Among the most important responsibilities a principal has is to restore those reasons for affirmation to the eyes, ears, minds, and hearts of everyone in the school. Put it in the form of a standing order:

UNTIL FURTHER NOTICE:
CELEBRATE
EVERYTHING

This means not just taking note of reasons to celebrate but actively looking for those reasons and then celebrating them. Find reasons. Create them, if necessary. Make time for them.

Consider instituting Shout-out Thursdays, in which everyone is invited to recognize the achievement, service, or good idea of someone in our building. Publish the news by text and through your social media accounts. Even broadcast the news over the PA. Whatever you do, make certain that homeroom teachers have the shout-out available to share with their students.

Proclaim a Teacher of the Month, with every student and every staff member invited to submit names.

Recognize every student's achievement. Do this at Merit Assemblies and Honor Roll Assemblies.

Celebrate test score increases, first-place accolades, weddings, and birthdays. If a student, teacher, or administrator makes it into the news for any positive achievement, ensure that everyone in the school community, parents included, knows about it. In fact, make it our business to collect and report and celebrate anything positive.

And get into the habit of kicking every piece of positive news upstairs, to the district and state administration. Principals must be unashamed cheerleaders for their schools.

Don't allow any achievement to slip by unnoticed, uncongratulated, or uncelebrated. Set as your standing goal to celebrate every student, every teacher, every parent, every administrator—out loud and in public—at least once in every semester. Find reasons to do so.

Anything good that happens? Celebrate it. Loudly.

Notes

PREFACE

1. Center for Labor Market Studies, "The Fiscal Economic Consequences of Cropping Out of High School" (Northeastern University, Boston), https://www.bostonpic.org/assets/resources/Research_Dropout_Key-Findings.pdf.

CHAPTER 1

1. D. Aguilar, Sean Kearney, and D. Herrington, *Beating the Odds: Exploring the 90/90/90 Phenomenon* (Philadelphia: Rutledge Taylor and Francis Group, 2012).

2. L. K. Bradshaw, "The changing role of principals in school partnerships," *NASSP Bulletin* (2000), *84*(616), 86–96; V. Dutta and S. Sabney, "School leadership and its impact on student achievement: The mediating role of school climate and teacher job satisfaction," *International Journal of Educational Management* (2016), *30*(6), 941–958; L. Darling-Hammond, "Third annual brown lecture in education research. The flat earth and education: How America's commitment to equity will determine our future," *Educational Researcher* (2007), *36*(6), 318–334, doi:10.3102/0013189x07308253; K. Leithwood and D. Jantzi, "Transformational leadership," *Leadership and Policy in Schools* (2005), *4*(3), doi:10.4324/9781410617095; J. Quin, A. Bischoff, and J. Johnson, "Comparison of transformational leadership practices: Implications for school districts and principal preparation," *Journal of Leadership Education* (2015), *14*(3), doi:10.12806/v14/i3/r5.

3. L. Drysdale, D. Gurr, and H. Goode, "Dare to make a difference: Successful principals who explore the potential of their role," *ISEA* (2016), 44;

Dutta & Sahney, 2016; J. Sebastian and E. Allensworth, "The influence of principal leadership on classroom instruction and student learning: A study of mediated pathways of learning," *Educational Administration Quarterly* (2012), *48*(4), 626–663, doi: 10.1177/0013161X11436273; K. A. White-Smith and M. A. White, "High school reform implementation," *Urban Education* (2008), *44*(3), 259–279, doi:10.1177/0042085909333942: P. Hallinger, "Leading educational change: Reflections on the practice or instructional and transformational leadership," *Cambridge Journal of Education* (2003), *33*(3), 329–352, doi:10.1080/0305764032000122005; J. Sebastian, H. Huang, and E. Allensworth, "Examining integrated leadership systems in high schools: Connecting principal and teacher leadership to organizational processes and student outcomes," *School Effectiveness and School Improvement* (2017), *28*(3), 463–488, doi:10.1080/09243453.2017.1319392; R. H. Shatzer, P. Caldarella, P. R. Hallam, and B. L. Brown, "Comparing the effects of instructional and transformational leadership on student achievement," *Educational Management Administration & Leadership* (2013), *42*(4), 445–459.

4. Dutta and Sahney, 2016; T. Ford, *Culturally Responsive Leadership: How One Principal in an Urban Primary School Responded Successfully to Maori Student Achievement* (NGA ARA RAP Matauranga-Maori Education, 2012), 28–35; Shatzer et al., 2013; White-Smith, 2012.

5. J. Hyman, "Can all-male high schools boost African American Boys' graduation rates?" *The Village Voice* (2009). Retrieved from https://www.villagevoice.com/2009/07/28/can-all-male-high-schools-boost-african-american-boys-graduation-rates/.

6. C. A. Warren, *Urban Preparation: Young Black Men Moving from Chicago's South Side to Success in Higher Education* (Cambridge, MA: Harvard Education Press, 2017).

7. K.A. White-Smith, "Beyond instructional leadership: The lived experiences of principals in successful urban schools," *Journal of School Leadership* (2012), *22*, 6–24; T. Ford, *Culturally Responsive Leadership: How One Principal in an Urban Primary School Responded Successfully to Maori Student Achievement* (NGA ARA RAPU Matauranga-Maori Education, 2012), 28–35.

8. Ford, 2012; P. A. Noguera, "The 2007 Charles H. Thompson lecture-colloquium presentation: Creating schools where race does not predict achievement: The role and significance of race in the racial achievement gap," *The Journal of Negro Education* (2008), *77*(2), 90–103; Shatzer et al., 2013; White-Smith, 2012.

9. White-Smith, 2012.

10. Schott Foundation for Public Education, *The Urgency of Now: The Schott 50 State Report on Public Education and Black Males* (2015). Retrieved from http://www.schottfoundation.org/urgency-of-now.pdf.

11. K. David and G. Marchant, "The achievement gaps in the United States: Race, poverty, and interactions over ten years," *The International Journal of Assessment and Evaluation* (2015), *22*(4), 1–15, doi:10.18848/2327-7920/cgp/v22i04/48378.

12. Unless otherwise noted, interviews with high school principals were conducted by the author and were first used in M. E. Abraham, "An examination of principal practices and successful outcomes for Black male high school students," diss., Ralph C. Wilson, Jr. School of Education, St. John Fischer College (August 2019). To protect the privacy of the interviewees, both their names and the names of their schools are pseudonyms.

13. J. Saldaña, *The Coding Manual for Qualitative Researchers*, 3rd ed. (Washington, DC: Sage Publications Inc., 2016).

14. Saldaña, 2016.

15. K. Leithwood and D. Jantzi, "Transformational leadership," *Leadership and Policy in Schools* (2016), *4*(3), doi: 10.4324/9781410617095; Shatzer et al., 2013.

CHAPTER 2

1. M. Roderick, "What's happening to the boys? Early high school experiences and school outcomes among African American male adolescents in Chicago," *Urban Education* (2003), *38*(5), 538–607, doi:10.1177/0042085903256221

2. M. A. Khalifa, M. A. Gooden, and J. E. Davis, "Culturally responsive school leadership: A synthesis of the literature," *Review of Educational Research* (2016), *86*(4), 1272–1311.

3. M. Tyler, F. Thompson, D. Gat, J. Burris, H. Lloyd, and S. Fisher, "Internalized stereotypes and academic self-handicapping among Black American male high school students," *Educational, School & Counseling Psychology* (2016), *67*, 1–4.

4. A. Jeffers, "Reflections of Academic experiences from formerly incarcerated African American Males," *Equity & Excellence in Education* (2017), *50*(2), 222–240; Jeffers's findings are somewhat contradictory to another study that suggested that students who eventually dropped out of school performed more poorly in lower grades like kindergarten: G. P. Hickman, M. Bartholomew, and R. Heinrich, "Differential developmental pathways of high school dropouts and graduates," *The Journal of Educational Research* (2008), *102*(1). This quantitative study examined the developmental pathways between high school graduates and dropouts. Hickman et al. suggested that students who drop out of school demonstrated signs of dropping out by their reading levels in third grade.

5. M. Lynn, J. Nicole-Bacon, T. Totten, T. Bridges, and M. Jennings, "Examining teacher's beliefs about African American male students in a low performing high

school in an African American school district," *Teachers College Record* (2010), *112*, 289–330.

6. Lynn et al., 2010; Tyler et al., 2016; Roderick, 2003.

7. P. A. Noguera, "The 2007 Charles H. Thompson Lecture-Colloquium Presentation: Creating schools where race does not predict achievement: The role and significance of race in the racial achievement gap," *The Journal of Negro Education* (2008), *77*(2), 90–103.

8. Noguera, 2008.

9. Khalifa et al., 2016; Roderick, 2003.

10. J. Sebastian, H. Huang, and E. Allensworth, "Examining integrated leadership systems in high schools: Connecting principal and teacher leadership to organizational processes and student outcomes," *School Effectiveness and School Improvement* (2017), *28*(3), 463–488, doi:10.1080/09243453.2017.1319392; Roderick, 2003; E. O. McGee, "Threatened and placed at risk: High achieving African American males in urban high schools," *The Urban Review* (2013), *45*(4), 448–471. , doi:10.1007/s11256-013-0265-2

11. A. Darensbourg, E. Perez, and J. Blake, "Overrepresentation of African American males in exclusionary discipline: The role of school-based mental health professionals in dismantling the school to prison pipeline," *Journal of African American Males in Education* (2010), *1*(3).

12. Schott, 2015.

13. L. Thompson and J. Davis, "The meaning high-achieving African American males in an urban high school ascribe to mathematics," *The Urban Review* (2013), *45*(4), 490–517, doi:10.1007/s11256-013-0267-0

14. Thompson and Davis, 2013; B. E. Pringle, J. E. Lyons, and K. C. Booker, "Perceptions of teacher expectations by African American high school students," *The Journal of Negro Education* (2010), *79*(1), 33–40.

15. Thompson and Davis, 2013.

16. Pringle et al., 2010.

17. Schott, 2015.

18. Thompson and Davis, 2013; McGee, 2013.

19. McGee, 2013; Thompson and Davis, 2013; Pringle et al., 2010.

20. R. Skiba and M. Rausch, "Zero tolerance, suspension, and expulsion: Questions of equity and effectiveness," *Handbook of classroom management: Research, practice, and contemporary issues* (Mahwah, NJ: Lawrence Erlbaum Associates Publishers, 2006).

21. S. Davis, H. Davis, and L. Darling-Hammond, "Innovative principal preparation programs: What works and how we know," *Planning and Changing* (2012), *43*, 25–45.

22. Davis, Davis, and Darling-Hammond, 2012.

23. K. T. Backor and S. P. Gordon, "Preparing principals as instructional leaders," *NASSP Bulletin* (2015), *99*(2), 105–126. doi:10.1177/0192636515587353; Davis, Davis, and Darling-Hammond, 2012.

24. Backor and Gordon, 2015; J. Quin, A. Deris, G. Bischoff, and J. Johnson, "Comparison of transformational leadership practices: Implications for school districts and principal preparation," *Journal of Leadership Education* (2015), *14*(3). doi:10.12806/v14/i3/r5; and J. Kouzes and B. Posner, *The Leadership Challenge*, 4th ed. (San Francisco: Jossey-Bass, 2007).

25. Quin et al., 2015.

CHAPTER 4

1. Peter Dolton, Oscar Marcenaro, Robert de Vries, and Po-Wen She, "Global teacher status: Index 2018," Varkey Foundation, Retrieved from https://www.var keyfoundation.org/media/4867/gts-index-13-11-2018.pdf.

2. Center for Labor Market Studies, "The fiscal economic consequences of cropping out of high school," Northeastern University, Boston, Retrieved from https://www.bostonpic.org/assets/resources/Research_Dropout_Key-Findings.pdf.

CHAPTER 6

1. AdlerPedia: All Things Adlerian, Retrieved from https://www.adlerpedia.org/concepts/127.

CHAPTER 7

1. Tom Peters, "What gets measured gests done," Retrieved from https://tompete rs.com/columns/what-gets-measured-gets-done/.

CHAPTER 10

1. Edmund Morris, *The Rise of Theodore Roosevelt* (1979; reprinted, New York: The Modern Library, 2001), Chapter 2; Kindle edition.

CHAPTER 11

1. Tyrone C. Howard, *Black Male(d): Peril and Promise in the Education of African American Males* (New York and London: Teachers College, Columbia University, 2014), 48.

CHAPTER 12

1. Rod Watson, "McKinley principal overcame obstacles to teach—as job hangs in the balance," *The Buffalo News*, Retrieved August 28, 2019, from https://buffalo news.com/opinion/columnists/mckinley-principal-overcame-obstacles-to-teach-as-jo b-hangs-in-balance/article_72cdce9b-d3fa-5de6-9617-33ec93f2e02d.html.
2. Laura M. Maruschak and Todd D. Minton, "Correctional populations in the United States 2017–2018," *Bureau of Justice Statistics*, Retrieved August 27, 2020, from https://www.bjs.gov/index.cfm?ty=pbdetail&iid=7026.

References

Adamson, F., & Darling-Hammond, L. (2012). Funding disparities and the inequitable distribution of teachers: Evaluating sources and solutions. *Education Policy Analysis Archives, 20*, 37. doi:10.14507/epaa.v20n37.2012

Aguilar, D., Kearney, S., & Herrington, D. (2012). *Beating the odds: Exploring the 90/90/90 phenomenon*. Philadelphia, PA: Rutledge Taylor & Francis Group.

Backor, K. T., & Gordon, S. P. (2015). Preparing principals as instructional leaders. *NASSP Bulletin, 99*(2), 105–126. doi:10.1177/0192636515587353

Big5 (2018). 2017 Overview and data. Retrieved from https://big5schools.org/budget legislative-issues/district-overview-data/

Blair, M. (2002). Effective school leadership: the multi-ethnic context. *British Journal of Sociology of Education, 23*(2), 179–191. doi:10.1080/01425690220137701

Blase, J., & Blase, J. (2000). Effective instructional leadership. *Journal of Educational Administration, 38*(2), 130–141. doi:10.1108/09578230010320082

Bradshaw, L. K. (2000). The changing role of principals in school partnerships. *NASSP Bulletin, 84*(616), 86–96.

Brinkmann, S. (2015). *Interviews learning the craft of qualitative research interviewing*. Thousand Oaks, CA: Sage Publications Inc.

Bristol, T. J. (2014). Teaching boys: Towards a theory of gender-relevant pedagogy. *Gender and Education, 27*(1), 53–68. doi:10.1080/09540253.2014.986067

Creswell, J. (2007). *Qualitative inquiry and research design*. Thousand Oaks, CA: Sage Publications Inc.

Creswell, J. (2014). *Research design qualitative, quantitative and mixed methods approaches*. Thousand Oaks, CA: Sage Publications Inc.

Darensbourg, A., Perez, E., & Blake, J. (2010). Overrepresentation of African American males in exclusionary discipline: The role of school-based mental health professionals in dismantling the school to prison pipeline. *Journal of African American Males in Education, 1*(3), 196–210.

Darling-Hammond, L. (2007). Third annual Brown lecture in education research. The flat earth and education: How America's commitment to equity will determine our future. *Educational Researcher, 36*(6), 318–334. doi:10.3102/0013189x07308253

David, K., & Marchant, G. (2015). The achievement gaps in the United States: Race, poverty, and interactions over ten years. *The International Journal of Assessment and Evaluation, 22*(4), 1–15. doi:10.18848/2327-7920/cgp/v22i04/48378

Davis, S. H., & Darling-Hammond, L. (2012). Innovative principal preparation programs: What works and how we know. *Planning and Changing, 43*, 25–45.

Drysdale, L., Gurr, D., & Goode, H. (2016). Dare to make a difference: Successful principals who explore the potential of their role. Paper presented at University Council of Educational Administration, Denver, November 2012, 1–16.

Dutta, V., & Sahney, S. (2016). School leadership and its impact on student achievement: The mediating role of school climate and teacher job satisfaction. *International Journal of Educational Management, 30*(6), 941–958.

Dweck, C. S. (2006). *Mindset: The new psychology of success.* New York, NY: Random House.

Eisenstadt, M. (2017). Syracuse city school district is N0. 1 for number of homeless students in the state outside of NYC. Retrieved from Syracuse.com

Fantuzzo, J., LeBeouf, W., Rouse, H., & Chen, C. (2012). Academic achievement of African American boys: A city-wide, community-based investigation of risk and resilience. *Journal of School Psychology, 50*, 559–579.

Finnigan, K. S. (2012). Principal leadership in low-performing schools. *Education and Urban Society, 44*(2), 183–202. doi:10.1177/0013124511431570

Fletcher, E. C., & Cox, D. E. (2012). Exploring the meaning African American students ascribe to their participation in high school career academics and in challenges they experience. *The High School Journal, 96*(1), 4–19.

Ford, T. (2012). *Culturally responsive leadership: How one principal in an urban primary school responded successfully to Maori student achievement.* NGA ARA RAPU Matauranga-Maori Education, 28–35.

Graham, A., & Anderson, K. A. (2008). I have to be three steps ahead; academically gifted African American male students in an urban high school tension between ethnic and academic identity. *The Urban Review, 40*(5), 472–499. doi:10.1007/s11256-008-0088-8

Gregory, A., Skiba, R. J., & Noguera, P. A. (2010). The achievement gap and the discipline gap. *Educational Researcher, 39*(1), 59–68. doi:10.3102/0013189x09357621

Hallinger, P. (2003). Leading educational change: Reflections on the practice of instructional and transformational leadership. *Cambridge Journal of Education, 33*(3), 329–352. doi:10.1080/0305764032000122005

Hallinger, P., Bickman, L., & Davis, K. (1996). School context, principal leadership, and student reading achievement. *The Elementary School Journal, 96*(5), 527–549. doi:10.1086/461843

Harper, S. R. (2009). Niggers no more: A critical race counternarrative on Black male student achievement at predominantly White colleges and universities. *International Journal of Qualitative Studies in Education, 22*(6), 697–712. doi:10.1080/09518390903333889

Heifetz, R., & Linsky, M. (2002). A survival guide for leaders. *Harvard Business Review, 80*(6):65–74, 152. Retrieved from https://hbr.org/2002/06/a-survival-guide-for-leaders

Hickman, G. P., Bartholomew, M., Mathwig, J., & Heinrich, R. (2008). Differential developmental pathways of high school dropouts and graduates. *The Journal of Educational Research, 102*(1), 3–14.

Hodgetts, K. (2010). Boys' underachievement and the management of teacher accountability. *Discourse Studies in the Cultural Politics of Education, 31*(1), 29–43. doi:10.1080/01596300903465401

Horng, E. L., Klasik, D., & Loeb, S. (2009). Principal time-use and school effectiveness. *School Leadership Research Report No. 09-3*. Stanford, CA: Stanford University, Institute for Research on Education Policy & Practice.

Husband, T. (2014). Increasing reading engagement in African American boys. *Multicultural Learning and Teaching, 9*(2). doi:10.1515/mlt-2013-0002

Hyman, J. (2009). Can all-male high schools boost African American boys' graduation rates? *The Village Voice*. Retrieved from https://www.villagevoice.com/2009/07/28/can-all-male-high-schools-boost-african-american-boys-graduation-rates/.

Jantzi, D., & Leithwood, K. (1996). Towards and explanation of variation in teachers' perceptions of transformational school leadership. *Educational Administration Quarterly, 32*(4), 512–535.

Jeffers, A. (2017). Reflections of Academic experiences from formerly incarcerated African American Males. *Equity & Excellence in Education, 5*(2), 222–240.

Jones, L. (2015). *High school leaders' perceptions of practices that increase graduation rates for African American males.* (Doctoral Dissertation). Retrieved from ProQuest Dissertations and Theses database. (UM 10011534).

Kearney, W. S., Herrington, D. E., & Aguilar, D. V. (2012). Beating the odds: Exploring the 90/90/90 phenomenon. *Equity & Excellence in Education, 45*(2), 239–249. doi:10.1080/10665684.2012.661248

Khalifa, M. A., Gooden, M, A., & Davis, J, E. (2016). Culturally responsive school leadership: A synthesis of the literature. *Review of Educational Research, 86*(4), 1272–1311.

Kouzes, J., & Posner, B. (2007). *The leadership challenge* (4th ed.). San Francisco, CA: Jossey-Bass.

Kunjufu, J. (2004). *Countering the conspiracy to destroy Black boys.* Chicago, IL: African American Images.

Leithwood, K. (2005). Transformational leadership for challenging schools. *Orbit, 35*(3), 43–44.

Leithwood, K., & Jantzi, D. (1996). Toward an explanation of variation in teachers' perceptions of transformational school leadership. *Educational Administration Quarterly, 32*(4), 512–538.

Leithwood, K., & Jantzi, D. (2005). Transformational leadership. *Leadership and Policy in Schools, 4*(3). doi:10.4324/9781410617095

Lewis, S., Simon, C., Uzzell, R., Horwitz, A., & Casserly, M. (2010). *A call for change: The social and educational factors contributing to the outcomes of African American males in urban schools.* Washington, DC: The Council of the Great City Schools.

Lynn, M., Nicole-Bacon, J., Totten, T., Bridges, T., & Jennings, M. (2010). Examining teacher's beliefs about African American male students in a low performing high school in an African American school district. *Teachers College Record, 112*, 289–330.

Madhlangobe, L., & Gordon, S. P. (2012). Culturally responsive leadership in a diverse school: A case study of a high school leader. *NASSP Bulletin, 96*, 177–202. doi:10.1177/0192636512450909

McGee, E. O. (2013). Threatened and placed at risk: High achieving African American males in urban high schools. *The Urban Review, 45*(4), 448–471. doi:10.1007/s11256-013-0265-2

McGee, G. W. (2004) Closing the achievement gap: Lessons from Illinois' golden spike high-poverty high-performing schools. *Journal of Education for Students Placed at Risk (JESPAR), 9*(2), 97–125, doi:10.1207/s15327671espr0902_2

Meier, T. (2014). The brown face of hope. *The Reading Teacher, 68*(5), 335–343. doi:10.1002/trtr.1310

New York State Education at a Glance (n.d.). Retrieved from https://data.nysed.gov/

Noguera, P. A. (2008). The 2007 Charles H. Thompson Lecture-Colloquium Presentation: Creating schools where race does not predict achievement: The role and significance of race in the racial achievement gap. *The Journal of Negro Education, 77*(2), 90–103.

Noguera, P. A. (2012). Saving Black and Latino boys: What schools can do to make a difference. *Phi Delta Kappan, 93*(5), 8–12. doi:10.1177/003172171209300503

Obama, B. (2014). My Brother's Keeper. *Reclaiming Children and Youth, Blooming-ton, IL, 23*(1), 5–8.

Parr, A. K., & Bonitz, V. S. (2015). Role of family background, student behaviors, and school related beliefs in predicting high school dropouts. *Journal of Educational Research*, 504–514. doi:10.1080/0020671

Parsons, Felicia. (2017). An intervention for the intervention: Integrating positive behavioral interventions and supports with culturally responsive practices. *The Delta Kappa Gamma Bulletin: International Journal for Professional Educators*, *83*(3), 52–56.

Paterson, Gregory (2012). Separating the boys form the girls. *Phi Delta Kappan, 93*(5), 37–41. doi:149.69.257.57

Pringle, B. E., Lyons, J. E., & Booker, K. C. (2010). Perceptions of teacher expectations by African American high school students. *The Journal of Negro Education, 79*(1), 33–40.

Quin, J., Deris, A., Bischoff, G., & Johnson, J. (2015). Comparison of transformational leadership practices: Implications for school districts and principal preparation. *Journal of Leadership Education, 14*(3). doi:10.12806/v14/i3/r5

Rhoden, S. (2017). Trust me, you are going to college: How trust influences academic achievement in Black males. *The Journal of Negro Education, 86*(1), 52. doi:10.7709/jnegroeducation.86.1.0052

Robinson, Q., & Webflow, J. (2012). Beating the odds: How single Black mothers influence the educational success of their sons enrolled in failing schools. *American Secondary Education, 40*(2), 52–66.

Roderick, M. (2003). What's happening to the boys? Early high school experiences and school outcomes among African American male adolescents in Chicago. *Urban Education, 38*(5), 538–607. doi:10.1177/0042085903256221

Saldaña, J. (2016). *The coding manual for qualitative researchers* (3rd ed.). Washington, DC: Sage Publications Inc.

Schott Foundation for Public Education (2015). *The Urgency of Now: The Schott 50 State Report on Public Education and Black Males*. Retrieved from http://schottfoundation.org/report/urgency-now-schott-50-state-report-public-education-and-black-males

Sebastian, J., & Allensworth, E. (2012). The influence of principal leadership on classroom instruction and student learning; A study mediated pathways of learning. *Educational Administration Quarterly, 48*(4), 626–663. doi:10.1177/0013161X11436273

Sebastian, J., Huang, H., & Allensworth, E. (2017). Examining integrated leadership systems in high schools: Connecting principal and teacher leadership to organizational processes and student outcomes. *School Effectiveness and School Improvement, 28*(3), 463–488. doi:10.1080/09243453.2017.1319392

Shatzer, R. H., Caldarella, P., Hallam, P. R., & Brown, B. L. (2013). Comparing the effects of instructional and transformational leadership on student achievement. *Educational Management Administration & Leadership, 42*(4), 445–459.

Skiba, R., & Rausch, M. (2006). *Zero tolerance, suspension, and expulsion: Questions of equity and effectiveness. Handbook of classroom management: Research, practice, and contemporary issues.* Mahwah, NJ: Lawrence Erlbaum Associates Publishers.

Sun, J., & Leithwood, K. (2012). Transformational school leadership effects on student achievement. *Leadership and Policy in Schools, 11*(4), 418–451. doi:10.1080/15700763.2012.681001

Thompson, L., & Davis, J. (2013). The meaning high-achieving African American males in an urban high school ascribe to mathematics. *The Urban Review, 45*(4), 490–517. doi:10.1007/s11256-013-0267-0

Toldson, I. A., Fry Brown, R. L., & Sutton, R. M. (2009). Commentary: 75 years after the "mis-education of the Negro": New imperatives for the education of Black males. *The Journal of Negro Education, 78*(3), 195–203.

Tschannen-Moran, M., & Gareis, C. R. (2015). Faculty trust in the principal: An essential ingredient in high-performing schools. *Journal of Educational Administration, 53*(1), 66–92. doi:10.1108/jea-02-2014-0024

Tyler, M., Thompson, F., Gat, D., Burris, J., Lloyd, H., & Fisher, S. (2016). Internalized stereotypes and academic self-handicapping among Black American male high school students. *Educational, School & Counseling Psychology, 67*, 1–4.

Tyre, P. (2008). *The trouble with boys a surprising report card on our sons, their problems at school, and what parents and educators must do.* New York, NY: Crown Publishing Group.

Versland, T. (2013). Principal efficacy: Implications for rural "grow your own" leadership programs. *Rural Educator, 35*(1). doi:ISSN-0273-446X

White-Smith, K. A. (2012). Beyond instructional leadership: The lived experiences of principals in successful urban schools. *Journal of School Leadership, 22*, 6–24.

White-Smith, K. A., & White, M. A. (2008). High school reform implementation. *Urban Education, 44*(3), 259–279. doi:10.1177/0042085909333942

Index

About the Author

Dr. Marck Abraham is the founder and CEO of MEA Consulting Services, LLC, which he designed to help poorly performing schools and organizations increase achievement for all students, especially young men of color.

As a thought leader for men of color, author, and motivational speaker, Dr. Abraham has presented to various education audiences and school districts in New York and across the country. Abraham's strategies for increasing graduation rates for males of color have been featured in SREB's *Promising Practices Newsletter*, the *Buffalo News*, and on local radio. He has been recognized by the mayor of Buffalo, New York, as one of the top principals in the city of Buffalo. McKinley High School, where he was principal, has been cited by New York State Education Department for having one of the highest graduation rates for males of color in New York. Dr. Abraham has taken a graduation rate, which hovered around the 60s when he first arrived at the school in 2014, to 87 percent and a 93 percent graduation rate for Black males in 2020. As the superintendent of Buffalo noted, Dr. Abraham drove "one of the highest graduation rates in the school's history."

Author photo courtesy of Yves-Richard Blanc, Blanc Photographie.